Changing Towards Excellence

a toolkit for transformational leaders of schools

Changing Towards Excellence

a toolkit for transformational leaders of schools

John R Rowling

tb

Trentham Books

Stoke on Trent and Sterling, USA

Trentham Books Limited

Westview House	22883 Quicksilver Drive
734 London Road	Sterling
Oakhill	VA 20166-2012
Stoke on Trent	USA
Staffordshire	
England ST4 5NP	

First published 2003

British Library Cataloguing-in-Publication Data
A catalogue record for this book is available from the British Library

ISBN 1 85856 314 3

Designed and typeset by Trentham Print Design Ltd., Chester and printed in Great Britain by Bemrose Shafron (Printers) Ltd., Chester.

Contents

It is not the strongest of the species that survives, nor the most intelligent, but the one most responsive to change.
Charles Darwin

At times our own light goes out and is rekindled by a spark from another person. Each of us has cause to think with deep gratitude of those who have lighted a flame within us.
Albert Schweitzer

Acknowledgements

I want to say thank you to some people that I know, and many that I do not know, for lighting the flame within me.

To all the staff at Nunthorpe School who have been my inspiration; over the years many of them moved on to promotion; we missed them, but we were encouraged by their ambition to further excellence in their own right. Amongst them Stephen and Dee, both now excellent leaders themselves; always remembered with the utmost affection and appreciation; your ambition and commitment kept me on my toes and challenged me to lead with purpose and clarity.

To Wyll, David, Alma, Andrew, Hermione, Nic, Arnold and Louise who have been the curriculum team most recently engaged with me in the pursuit of excellence, ever open to change and eager to influence, so that a difference can be made with young people. Your ability to continue to raise the standard ever higher has been wonderful to behold.

To David, Seana, Sharron, Neil and David, brilliant pastoral leaders, prepared to expend energy and time, dedicated to service and betterment: your enterprise, passion and care has been excellent.

To Pat and her team of loving, caring, compassionate, skilful and dedicated staff in Effective Learning; you ought to be proud of what you achieve. You give young people safety, security, self-esteem, opportunity, courage and faith, and they grow, develop and achieve amazing things. Your work has been one of my greatest joys. Mia has been a wonderful addition to a tremendous team.

To Kathy and Barry, supportive and encouraging, wise and compassionate, I owe a great deal more than I can say. Your loyalty has been humbling, your kindness and professionalism remarkable. Thank you so much for it all.

To Ian Click, chair of governors, relentless in the pursuit of excellence yourself and dedicated to the constant progress of the school. Without your quiet persistence I would never have embarked on this journey. I have appreciated your support, insight, determination and ambition, all with respect for our differing roles. You have fanned the flame in me more times than I can recall.

To Ann and Ann, riding into a happy sunset with me, I owe an immense debt of gratitude. Your skill, experience, patience, loyalty and generosity of spirit have been a daily source of strength. What you do not know about the school is barely worth knowing. Your talents and warm-hearted support will be sorely missed, but will remain always in my memory.

To Dave and his team of technicians who appear able to answer every question, and to do magic with technology, I owe a great deal. Your personal growth towards excellence has been inspiring to watch. I am proud of you.

To all the remaining staff, too many to mention one by one: you have put up with my idiosyncracies for a very long time with good grace, most of the time. You laugh at me, but more often with me, you sometimes cry with me, you share the vision, you generated the momentum and did very little to slow it down. You made the school what it has become. You deserve great credit and much appreciation. Your names are not written here, but they are in my heart.

To countless students who have passed through our doors: you soon convinced me that, with sufficient inspiration, there were few limitations to what you could achieve: seeking to encourage that inspiration has been as big a challenge as any one could want. From you I have learned so much.

To Jenny Vickers who continues to be a source of inspiration: your interest in what we do, long after there was any need to show it, has been such an encouragement. Your experience, wisdom, grace and dignity will doubtless be as successful in York as they were in Redcar and Cleveland. You have a remarkable ability to draw the best out of professionals: you certainly had that effect on me.

To Patrick; long-time friend and colleague; it was impossible to fall out with you even when we disagreed. Thank you for all your help and encouragement in the earlier years of my developing leadership; it was appreciated. Your comments on the draft of my first book gave me the confidence to press on. Thank you.

To Jenny Lewis: thank you for your interest, support and leadership and the time you give to the school. I am sorry our paths did not merge earlier because it has been a joy to work with you.

To Michael Fullan, who I have met only once: your writing has helped me see the power of the pen. Your work has created change in me and in my practice; your insight and ability to explain complexity in simple terms has inspired me. I am so grateful to have had the one chance to tell you that face to face.

To all the colleagues on the Leadership Network at the National College for School Leadership: on our introductions I found it humbling to hear what everybody else had done! When we met it was soon obvious that it was not just rhetoric. Thank you for helping me with some research for this book, and for your contributions. I have every confidence that with leaders like you around education is in good hands.

To Nick, Brenda, Chris, Jim, Hilary, Ray, Mo, Sheila, John, Stuart, Norma, Margaret, Alan and Sue: thank you for case study material, too much to be included in total but all helpful in the process of my work. Finding time for peripheral matters is not easy: I appreciated your willingness, indeed in some cases, eagerness, to be involved.

To Gillian: second time round was easier than the first because I knew you were there. Your brilliance in the use of words was a real comfort to one whose business for years was in dealing with numbers! I was confident that the final version of this book would be better than the draft because it had gone through the refinement of your mind.

To Nick and Rachel: you know we love you and are proud of you. What you are has been a delight to us and what you are becoming is a source of joy.

Talking of lighting fires leads me to Sheila my wife who nearly thirty years ago lit a fire in me that has never wavered nor flickered. You have been a model of support, taking interest in Nunthorpe well beyond the call of duty, feeling compassion and sensitivity for people you barely know. What I have been involved with has always had your full support. Any success I may have had, you must never doubt, has been, in no small measure because of your love, loyalty, support and strength. Your faith, and our faith, has been a source of immense inspiration; more than words could ever say. We know to whom the praise is due.

Introduction

When I wrote *Heading Towards Excellence* I blamed my chair of governors. He did lean on me quite hard but I have had cause to be grateful. This time I have only myself to blame. Three things have influenced me to write *Changing Towards Excellence*:

First, I have become absorbed by the subject of leadership, to the point where I have read more about it in the last two years than in all the previous thirty eight years I have been a teacher. Michael Fullan's work has been so influential, so clearly written, so full of wisdom and insight – so good in fact that it makes me hesitate to write on the subject myself. More recently, I have been challenged by the work of Jim Collins and John Kotter and been amazed to find that academics of their standing are saying things in which I have believed for some time. My approach is nothing like as academic as theirs, but it is based in the reality of my own experiences and this may give it some weight.

Second, I have been inspired by the response to *Heading Towards Excellence*. If I had never intended to write a book neither had I ever considered that its influence would extend so far. I have been told that if you sell over a thousand books of this type it is rated a 'best seller'; *Heading Towards Excellence* has sold many more than that. That feels good, but what is much more special is to discover that *Heading Towards Excellence* is being used by people who I did not even know had bought it. Some of them write to me with encouragement and appreciation, others invite me to hold conferences or training courses

with them. It has been difficult to do much of that because I am still trying hard to run a successful school but, when I have, I have learned as much from delegates as they have from me. It has been most rewarding and, now that retirement is imminent, maybe there will be opportunity to do so much more. After forty years in teaching, and nineteen as a headteacher, I hope to be able to give something back to a service from which I have gained so much. This book is intended to be a part of that process.

Heading Towards Excellence was about moving from good to exceptional: after nineteen years there is still some way to go. The process fascinates me and the challenge confronts me day by day. However, personal excellence is one aspiration, the ability to make transformational change in an organisation, in company with many others, quite another. Lord Salisbury asked, 'Who wants change? Things are bad enough as they are.' Perhaps that is a politician's perspective: I know, however, that students and parents want change, the government wants change and I want change, but only if it is going to make things better. Not all change does. From that background I came to study the change process within the educational world I know so well and discovered the seven processes outlined in this book. Hopefully they will be helpful to those involved at all levels of leadership because the principles are true whether you are a headteacher, a deputy or assistant headteacher, head of department or a team leader. From my work on *Heading Towards Excellence*, I have discovered that the principles extend well beyond education, having applications in any area where people want to improve: though this book has specific application to education, I believe the same is true of *Changing Towards Excellence*.

Peter Drucker once observed that 'people refer to gurus because they don't know how to spell charlatan'. I am grateful never to have been clever enough to be regarded as a guru, but I hope my experiences in life mean that neither can I be seen as a charlatan. This book is the by-product of my own learning, which I hope, in turn, will prove a great benefit to others working so hard in the wonderful world of education.

E. B. White of the *New Yorker* wisely wrote,' The ability to learn is a defining characteristic of being human; the ability to continue learning is an essential skill of leadership.' I have been learning a long time and there is still so much to know. If you feel the same way, this book may help.

Chapter 1

No one is immune to change

Much has happened, little has changed.
wall graffiti, Stockton-on-Tees

No organisation today – large or small, local or global – is immune to change. Education is no different. There is a current emphasis in education on 'transformational leadership' and, of course, transformation means change. Tom Peters said,

> Excellent firms don't believe in excellence – only in constant improvement and constant change

Just like excellent firms, schools that aspire towards excellence make sure that change means improvement. That is not always the case: it is possible to throw away tried, tested and proven practice in search of a quick fix leading to anything but quality progress. The secret is to protect the best and at the same time search for further advances. Thought needs to be given before embarking on change. It is no good at all to embark on change projects if it proves to be that 'everything has changed except our way of thinking', and yet making time to think seems not to be regarded as a priority for leaders in education or, if it is, it is often swamped by activity and routine day to day requirements. Unless leaders take time to think they will be in danger of being involved in plenty of activity but with little progress. Edward de Bono (1999) described situations like this:

> Everything is fine. But the ship is still heading in the wrong direction

Leaders intent on transformation need to have the courage to stop and think.

Needs Time ← → Saves Time

Time needs to be managed so that creativity and thinking is not forfeited: quality time spent thinking about the progress of an organisation is likely to lead to better planning than spontaneous reactive approaches. The secret is to engage in thinking leading to meaningful activity. The Chinese proverb said that the man seeking to fell the huge tree spends 'twice the time sharpening the axe'.

For all the talk of transformational leadership, research reported by John Kotter of Harvard Business School reveals that 'fewer than 15% of companies have successfully transformed themselves'. It could be that many companies have never even attempted to make significant change, preferring the safety of the status quo but, whatever the reason, this is not overwhelming success and is a salutary warning that educational leaders are not bound to succeed. It is important to understand the change process. Michael Fullan, in his book *Leading in a Culture of Change* (2001), highlights five components of leadership that will be required in successful transformation:

- Moral purpose
- Understanding change
- Relationships
- Knowledge creation and sharing
- Coherence making.

All of these are vitally important but this book will concentrate on understanding change, on what the processes are that leaders need to embark upon to ensure that transformation is embedded in their organisation. That is not to say that this is the most important component. Moral

purpose, the inward desire to make a difference, the deep driving force within a leader, probably deserves the highest status but the practicalities of making a transformation happen demands thought, time and attention and is the subject of this book. There are clear principles that apply to all organisations and, for all its many differences, education can apply these principles too. However, whatever principles are agreed, the leader plays the key role and bears the responsibility for transformation within any organisation. Leaders are important.

Leaders are important

Leadership is a challenging and exciting occupation, though as Jack Welch (2001) commented

> Leadership has its pluses and minuses – but the good sure overwhelms the bad. The schedule is packed, with many a day blocked out in advance, yet every day manages to bring new crises that butcher your calendar. The days are crazy long, yet the hours race by. The job never leaves you no matter what you are doing.

As an outstanding leader at GEC for so long, he speaks as a happy, successful and fulfilled man. For those who feel, and indeed are, less successful, leadership can be

daunting
frightening
demoralising
dispiriting
frustrating.

However, those of us in leadership are increasingly aware that leaders do make the difference and many aspire after an understanding of what it takes to be the person whose impact on the school is positive and transformational. There are lessons to be learned from those who have translated principles into high achievement, whether in business, commerce, industry or education. The

Success does not mean you have to be burnt-out or boring

principles that bring success in one have significant applications in the others.

It is possible, indeed necessary, to be successful without living a life that is all work: this issue of life-work balance has to be managed too, otherwise we run the risk of burn-out or boredom. Charles Handy's wife said at the height of his success, 'I am glad you are so successful, but I just want you to know that you have become the most boring man I know'. Some price to pay. Handy, of course, learned the lesson and so should we.

For most of my working life I avoided school related work on Sundays: whichever day you choose to call the 'seventh day' does not matter; six days has always seemed to me to be a good plan for happy balanced living. It is a poor advertisement to middle managers when, though they respect the leader, they see little appeal in her lifestyle.

It was Handy who observed in the seventies that 'Leadership as a topic has a rather dated air about it'. How things have changed. Tony Blair in a speech to mark the opening of the National College for School Leadership (2002) said that 'there are few jobs as tough as being a head – and none more important.' There are few headteachers who cannot relate a multitude of illustrative stories about the tough issues, ill-disciplined students, the impact of changing social norms, unsupportive parents and so on, but there is a need, greater now than ever, to see the enormous opportunity and challenge open to school leaders and to rise to it so that transformation of education can makes its impact on the lives and futures of young people. That

is, I believe, the motivation of David Hopkins who wrote

> A critical factor in a school's performance is the quality of leadership. Where standards are high, it is a direct reflection on the quality of leadership and that of the management team. (*Times Educational Supplement,* September 2002)

It seems an obvious corollary to make leadership, and its improvement, the focus of concentration for a government whose ambition is to initiate successful change in its schools and to introduce transformational change. Hopkins, who is Director of Effectiveness and Standards at the Department for Education and Skills, stated in 2002 that '*Improving leadership will therefore be a key priority for the government over the coming year.*'

Headteachers ought not to be defensive – improving their leadership should be welcome. In March 2003 Charles Clarke said that, though the number of seriously incompetent heads was small,

> Where the head's the problem, he must not be allowed just to go along. The head must be taken out or heads of department moved. Both the governors and the local education authority have to be completely ruthless addressing the problem.

He was accused of 'misguided rhetoric' and making 'bellicose and unhelpful' comments. David Hart, general secretary of the National Association of Headteachers, believes 'there is hardly an incompetent head left in the system'. Sadly, that seems unlikely. If there is, something should be done about it as positively as possible but if all else fails 'moving them out' seems eminently reasonable. I do not suppose that parents of students in such a school would find that unreasonable. All are agreed, however, that such cases are relatively few and that there are many

All headteachers could improve and such a confession ought not to be interpreted as an admission of failure

more whose aspirations are to be part of successful transformation. It seems a pity that the broader statement by Hopkins about 'improving leadership' should have been turned into thoughts about removing incompetent heads. The two issues are linked but they are different.

Sometimes leaders do fail. Recently I talked with a leader in a school who had made a horrendous mistake: she had submitted the wrong examination paper title in her entry for 114 students. The error was discovered when the moderator asked why no work had been sent in for moderation. The warning came just in time, though the error cost over £4000 to put right. It took great courage to face up to such failure but she had it: she looked with her headteacher at how it had happened, what systems she was employing in her leadership that could lead to so grave a mistake and what might be done to ensure it never happened again. She researched best practice in the generic organisational areas of her role and grew immeasurably. Serious errors need not be the catalyst that makes a person want to change: the fact that a man wants to be fitter does not mean he is ill.

Heather Du Quesnay who leads the National College warmed to the leadership emphasis. She wrote in 2003

> Good leadership is key to the success of an organisation and all who work and learn within it and nowhere is this more important than in schools.

Unsurprisingly, leadership has become a central emphasis for NCSL too in 2003.

The government backed its own rhetoric with funding to transform leadership. It chose to do it largely through the generous Leadership Incentive Grant (LIG), focused on schools in Excellence in Cities (EiC) areas or in schools in challenging circumstances. The financial support is substantial and ought to make a huge difference; time will tell. What it does make clear is that the government is serious about its intentions. Sadly, the limited number of recipients due to such restricted eligibility has led to some schools, particularly primaries, feeling that they do not matter. If leadership is important it is important for all leaders. In due course it seems inevitable that such a strongly supportive idea for leadership will be extended to all. It seems sensible, if money is limited, to focus on areas where the biggest impact might be made.

There are inevitably some tough questions to be asked: the government has every right to expect that funding on this scale should make a difference:

- How is the money being targeted?
- Is it really addressing raising standards and leadership?
- How is the impact of spending being monitored?

Already there are disturbing signs that LIG money is being used creatively, a euphemism for 'not quite as the government intended'.

Leadership is different from management

Alongside the new emphasis on leadership, a clear distinction is beginning to be drawn between leadership and management. It needs making. It is easy for a headteacher to be caught up, sometimes unwittingly, in a never ending round of management issues; but the engine that drives change is leadership. John Maxwell drew the distinction this way

> Leadership is about influencing people, while management focuses on maintaining systems and processes.

It is possible to create a good school with a heavy management influence but without transformational leadership it will never become a great one. Management is a set of processes that can keep a complicated system of people and technology running smoothly, whereas leadership defines what the future should look like, aligns people with that vision, and brings inspiration to make it happen despite the obstacles. All schools *need* good management to flourish but the best have good leadership too.

The influential Michael Fullan wrote in 2002

> Leadership is to this decade what standards were to the last in terms of large school reform.

> Leadership is the set of strategies that will take us to large school reform and sustainability.

In a research article in *Leader to Leader* (1998), John P Kotter, professor in the Harvard Business School, reported on leading edge research on transformational leadership in areas of life outside of education. He believes that, for all the good intentions, fewer than 15% of those who attempt transformation are actually successful in achieving it: further, he points out that successful transformation puts emphasis of 70% on leadership and 30% on management. This should not be daunting and off-putting, rather it should be an incentive to understand and apply principles that are proven to produce change.

In his book *Good to Great* (2001), Jim Collins talks about business being run rather like a bus. Management spends a long time sorting out the passengers on the bus, keeping order, ensuring comfort; leadership spends rather longer on who is allowed on the bus in the first place, and where it is going. Order on the bus is important but nothing like as crucial as knowing where it is going.

Leadership then is different, and it is important. At the launch of the National College, Tony Blair gave four qualities that make good leaders

- *Building and sustaining trust in organisations to motivate and enable them to cope with rapid change*

- *Establishing a coherent sense of mission and purpose so that every one is clear where the school is going*

- *Building a team of senior managers who together lead the institution*

- *Pursuing decisively high standards on the basis that every student is capable of significant achievement.*

These qualities, and others, will have a significant place in the plan for transformational change following later in this book. Creating the climate, defining direction, building teams and setting and maintaining standards are the bedrock of transformational leadership. To make change happen these procedures must be made into a practical programme of action; too often they remain theories of interest, provoking animated discussion and little more. That is not transformation.

What is leadership?

Leadership necessarily **enables other people to get involved**. Harry Overstreet observed that 'the very essence of all power to influence lies in getting the other person to participate'; he who leads but has no followers is only taking a walk. Transformational leadership will not happen without the involvement of many people: how to engage them, inspire and enable them is not easy.

It is a common view, though an erroneous and dangerous one, that leaders have to have a certain type of

Ofsted inspections taught me that good leaders had a wide variety of personalities. All knew what they wanted to do to create a successful school and all could communicate that in different ways to their staff

personality or style, often called charismatic. This idea is exemplified by a remark attributed to Margaret Thatcher

> Being in power (leadership) is like being a lady. If you have to tell people you are, you aren't.

It's clever enough, but it is stereotypical. The implication, perhaps as misguided about women as about leaders, is that there is something that stands out about them that is self-evident, something you are born with: that's its danger. John Gardner (1990) wrote

> Research has demonstrated over and over again that we must not think too rigidly or mechanically about the attributes of leaders. The attributes required of a leader depend on the kind of leadership being exercised, the context and the nature of followers.

Peter Drucker (1996) was much more strident and dismissive

> Leadership personality,"leadership style,' and 'leadership traits' do not exist. Amongst the most effective leaders I have encountered and worked with in a half century, some locked themselves into their office and others were ultra-gregarious. Some were 'nice guys' and others stern disciplinarians. Some were quick and impulsive; others studied again and again and then took forever to come to

a decision. Some were warm, others remained aloof. Some were self-effacing to a fault – some were excruciatingly vain. Some were as austere in their private lives as a hermit in the desert; others were ostentatious and pleasure-loving. Some were good listeners, but amongst the most effective were a few loners who listened only to their inner voice. The ONE and ONLY personality trait the effective ones I have encountered did have in common was something they did not have; they had little or no 'charisma' and little use either for the term or what it signifies.

I prefer the view of Rudolph Guiliani (2002)

> Leadership does not simply happen. It can be taught, learned, developed.

Certainly, most really successful leaders have 'presence', some have style, panache and flair, but many have **nurtured their talent**, honed and refined it, read, studied and learned. Most have done it because they wanted to make a difference. In the world of sport, the range of personalities amongst leaders of football clubs shows that there is not only one style of leadership: Arsene Wenger and Alex Ferguson, Sir Bobby Robson and Sven-Goran Erickson could scarcely be more different: it is the same in politics, Mandela, Clinton, Thatcher, Churchill and Kennedy were clearly not from the same leadership mould. It has to be the same in school leadership.

Leaders have the ability to combine two straightforward functions. As John Adair put it, 'a leader is sometimes a Cattle Prodder, sometimes a Cheer Leader': two leadership skills of considerable importance here; **challenge and encouragement**. People in any organisation are going to need challenging and they are certainly going to need encouraging. Daniel Goleman (1996), whose book on emotional intelligence has had such profound impact, noted the combination of skills needed in successful leadership

> Gifted leadership occurs where heart and head – feeling and thought – meet. These are the wings that allow a leader to soar.

We all know what happens to the flight patterns of birds with one wing. The ethos within an organisation unbalanced in its emphases will be seriously detrimentally affected. A school with the emphasis exclusively on encouragement will be soft, gentle, supportive, cosy and comfortable: it may well also be sleepy, coasting and underachieving. If the emphasis is all on challenge, the school is likely to be active, buzzing, driving, focused and demanding: it may be frenetic, tense, uncomfortable and neurotic too. Balance is important.

Encoragement Support Gentleness Care	Challenge Targets Probing Questions Tension

The leader needs a wise head to know when and how to be a cattle prodder; challenge is important, knowing times and places to make it necessary. A soft and tender heart, an emotional wisdom that discerns the needs of others, is just as important. These are not simple matters; they are significant and need scrupulous attention.

Jack Welch identified the four Es of GEC leadership. They were:

- Energy levels
- Energising ability
- Edge
- Execution

Whatever the organisation, these are the issues that lead to transformation. Leadership is demanding, will take **personal energy**, will need time and dedication, single-mindedness and

commitment. The **ability to energise** others around common goals is clearly essential and the skills to do it can be learned. Energy is easily dissipated on peripheral issues so the more it can be harnessed the better. Someone once said that 'energy is a marvellous thing, what a pity to waste it on youth': leaders cannot afford to waste it anywhere.

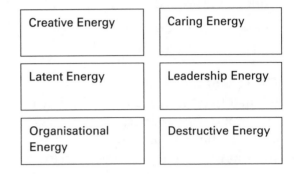

Creative Energy	Caring Energy
Latent Energy	Leadership Energy
Organisational Energy	Destructive Energy

According to scientists, energy can neither be created nor destroyed: it simply changes its forms. It can be dissipated, diverted or abused. Energy is productive: able to create light, warmth and movement but able also to destroy. It exists in every organisation in one form or another; the secret is in harnessing all that is available to produce life, vitality and productivity.

Edge is the **ability to make tough decisions**. One of the traditional competences of leaders was decisiveness. This is the Jack Welch Edge. Those who transform know how to be clear, direct and decisive. Larry Bossidy and Ram Charan called their latest book *Execution* (2002). Brought up as they were under the tutelage of Jack Welch before making their own way into corporate international leadership, they regard **the ability to make it happen** as the single most important quality a transformational leader can possess. This is what makes the difference. Leaders in schools share ideas, hear about initiatives, understand expectations, but the ability to make it happen distinguishes between those who transform and those who do not.

Rob Parsons, in his book *Heart of Success* (2002), writes that he is willing to sit in a conference all day for just one good idea. A bright idea is only as good as the power of the leader to make it happen in the particular circumstances of her own institution; there is an enormous gap between what seems like an excellent suggestion and finding how to make it work on the ground.

These are vital ingredients for success. And they can be learned.

The role of the leader

In order to transform an organisation a leader performs a variety of roles. First amongst them is **the art of communication**. There is so much to be communicated that learning when and how to do it best is of great significance. John Adair (2001) wrote

> Communicating aims, values or ideals of an organisation cannot be communicated on video or down-line. Face to face communication, preferably in small groups, cannot be beaten when it comes to changing the organisational culture.

Technology has many important uses, though, as Collins (2001) puts it, it is an accelerator of change rather than the cause of it. Almost always it is people who make the important transformations and in order to do that they need clear and, wherever possible, memorable and inspiring communication.

Communication is only as effective as the vision it communicates: transformation will not happen, even with the cleverest communication, if the vision is not clear. As part of a training session that I attended, participants were given the opportunity to outline their vision. The group was small. The first contributor began to explain the vision she had for her school. Twenty minutes later, amidst some embarrassment, the course leader

Many leaders make the vision too complicated. Keep it simple

interrupted. Clearly he had trouble understanding what sort of vision this was. How the staff of her school could make it out defies belief. Leaders spend hours, sometimes days, refining the vision statement of their organisation so that it is flawless, only to discover that few can remember it – even those who spent so much time writing it. The vital role of the leader is **to make sure that 'where we are going' is simple, clear and intelligible**. If it is also brief and succinct that is a bonus. Three of the simplest and clearest visions I have ever seen are those of Henry Ford, Wall-Mart and Walt Disney.

> I will build a motor car for the great multitude... It will be so low in price that no man making a good salary will be unable to own one and enjoy with his family the blessing of God's open spaces... – *Henry Ford*

> To give ordinary folk the chance to buy the same things as rich people. – *Wall-Mart*

> To make people happy. – *Walt Disney*

These visions seem to have worked well!

Graham Greene was once asked whether he regarded himself as a great novelist. 'Not great,' he said, 'but one of the best!' Transformational leaders will almost certainly **have aspirations** to make a mark and set their stall out to do so. They will not be prepared to settle for anything less than the best that they can achieve. Jim Collins observed

> We don't have great schools principally because we have good schools. Few people attain great lives in large part because it is so easy to settle for the good life.

It *is* easy: standards are acceptable, Ofsted causes no problems and league table performance is adequate; these matters are of small concern to the transformational leader who wants to move ever forward with aspirations to change towards excellence. One leader offered this advice and motivation, 'stretch beyond your limits, be better than you ever thought you could'.

No significant progress will be made in an organisation unless the workforce has positive self-esteem and a high degree of self-confidence. These are not characteristics that develop by good fortune. The transformational leader learns how **to maximise self-esteem and to develop self-confidence**. Jack Welch pointed out his belief that no good can arise '*when leaders lose their self-confidence, begin to panic, and spiral down into a hole of self-doubt.*' He advised 'watching this vortex' and warned his leaders to be careful when dealing with disciplinary matters within GEC. '*When people make mistakes, the last thing they need is discipline. It's time for encouragement and confidence building.*'

Welch knew the importance of this himself and attributes some of his own personal development to his mother's encouragement. He had a stammer that often embarrassed him. In his early years his mother used to say, 'It's because you're so smart. No one's tongue could keep up with a brain like yours.' Transformational leadership requires attention to be paid to promote well being in staff, to deal with difficult and complex matters with sensitivity in a spirit of encouragement. Again, these are skills that can be learned, nurtured and developed. No workers are going to change much if they feel they are being sucked down the plughole. The vortex must be avoided.

Most people will not change their patterns of behaviour if they have no cause to question what they are doing. Peter Drucker has an international reputation as the father of modern leadership theory. As well as writing best selling books, he has worked extensively as a consultant for many years. He is an expert on questioning and makes an art form of it. This is how he puts it

> The contribution I make to a client is basically to be very stupid and dense; ask simple, fundamental questions; demand that she be thoughtful with the answers; and demand that she makes decisions on what is important. I feel very strongly that a client who leaves my office feeling that she has learned a lot that she did not know before is a stupid client; either that, or I have not done my job. She leaves my office saying, 'I know all this – but why haven't I done anything about it?

Transformational leaders learn what questions to ask themselves, or they find a consultant who will help them to do so. What is more, they learn how **to ask probing questions of others**, which leaves them feeling good about themselves, having discovered a way forward even though they wonder why they had not seen it before.

Jim Collins differentiated between management and leadership with his illustration of the bus. He emphasised that who is on the bus is all important and argued that transformational leaders set the priority as getting the right people on the bus. In education it is difficult to get the wrong people off the bus. We saw how even *suggesting* 'taking people out' aroused considerable criticism of Charles Clarke. Collins' emphasis, however, is much more about having the best people in place and not taking on anyone who is not going to prove capable of working towards transformational leadership. Jack Welch categorised the leaders across the GEC organisation A, B or C and calculated on a spread of 20 / 70 / 10. It must have been uncomfortable to be classified as C! Of those in the top 20 % Jack used to say

Love 'em
Hug 'em
Kiss 'em
But
Don't lose 'em.

He argued that what made GEC an outstanding company was the way it encouraged, supported, celebrated, recognised and promoted the leaders who showed transformational leadership. People were promoted from GEC to head their own large companies but not before GEC could afford to let them go. Staff were regarded as a prize asset, and acknowledged and honoured. The best leaders **learn how to recognise potential, how to develop and encourage it and how to reward and celebrate it**. They learn how to develop loyalty and release all the creative power latent in people who feel valued.

The right people are likely to have distinctive qualities:

- outstanding interpersonal relationships
- evident moral purpose, discretely held
- energy that is highly focused
- a record of success in smaller projects
- ability to engage others – a team builder
- inspirational to colleagues
- wanting always to learn and progress, with fascination with betterment
- a real but realistic love of people
- ready to risk but not recklessness
- an inner conviction about what really matters to them
- the common touch

Collaboration is only successful when all involved having something worthwhile to offer want to share with others and have the skills to collaborate confidently. Too many people fail to see collaboration as an active process

Some entrepreneurs, Simon Cowell and Pete Waterman being classic examples in popular music, make a fortune from spotting talent: the future of education depends on existing leaders being able to recognise talent when they see it and then to nurture that talent.

Leaders like Jack Welch seemed able to **generate loyalty and commitment** and to inspire professional pride in the key people in the leadership team. It was 'one for all and all for one'. Though his company had many constituent parts, he had inculcated into the various team leaders that each had responsibility for the others as well as a commitment to their own. He wrote,

> I could not stand the idea of the company sinking and one of its parts making it to shore.

In 2003 the new word in education is 'collaboration'. The Leadership Incentive Grant holders are expected to develop plans collaboratively. By one definition, collaboration has treachery associations; that was not what the government had in mind! Rather the intention is that we should be all for one and one for all: that if schools in an LEA sink, the others could not stand the thought of it if one of them made it to shore. It is a powerful concept. However, collaboration works best when there is heart felt commitment; forced collaboration could provoke treachery.

Within a school, transformational change happens as a consequence of the actions of many parts; GEC is no different in that respect to schools. The transformational leader works on developing pride, involvement and heart for the organisation so for them too it is one for all and all for one. She takes no pride in the possibility that the school sinks yet one faculty makes it to shore. That positive ethos develops a momentum all of its own – it is wonderful to work in it.

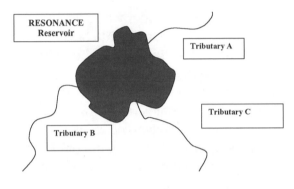

Daniel Goleman defined such an atmosphere as *Resonance*, a *reservoir of positivity* in the workplace where people prosper and thrive. It is the opposite of *toxicity*, poison, where little thrives, grows, flourishes or prospers. Michael Fullan's key theme of 'Relationships' links closely to resonance. But reservoirs have to be filled. During the course of day-to-day school and business life the waters are drained. The streams into the reservoir need to be kept free, clean, pure and wholesome. Pollutants can emerge in any organisation that will foul up the waters. Transformational leaders **guard the tributaries**.

Readers will work out for themselves what the tributaries are in their organisation. In schools they can be:

goodwill
teamwork
sharing
encouragement
self-discipline
commitment
trustworthiness

These are fragile environmental characteristics and a transformational leader needs an environment watch to protect the interests of the change she is seeking to engender.

The poison is often easy to discern but difficult to remove. Self-centredness, harsh and unkind criticism, gossip, jealousy, envy, malice, extreme competitiveness, laziness, resistance to change, uncooperativeness and treachery are all poisonous and will hinder the potential for transformation.

In a faculty I know well one member of staff was inclined to gossip and stir trouble behind people's backs. The Head of Faculty became aware of this and challenged it on the grounds that it was damaging the team spirit that she deemed essential to transformational change. It took three attempts to sort the matter out but it was resolved and significant transformation has taken place since.

The first of Michael Fullan's five great themes is Moral Purpose. The role of a leader is **to understand her Moral Purpose and to encourage and develop it in others**. It is odd how often resistance to the concept of Moral Purpose is encountered, usually on the grounds that morality is a private business. This is to totally misunderstand the concept as defined by Fullan, which seems to me to be beyond dispute. He categorises Moral Purpose in five ways

Headteachers hold beliefs and moral values but often do not communicate them

being deeply passionate about improving life
being intensely committed to betterment
making a difference in the lives of students
improving the quality of how we live together
anchoring practice in beliefs and values.

Transformational leaders will have worked out their own definition of Moral Purpose. Most headteachers I have worked with have been happy to accept that proposed by Fullan but, more surprisingly, conceded that this was not an issue to which they had given much thought for a long time. The twelfth competence of the assessment centres conducted for headteachers and deputies a few years ago was 'educational values'. Those assessors, who worked with NEAC, claimed that 'educational values' was the area in which responses from participants was weakest. It may have been more to do with testing mechanisms than the realities of headteacher perceptions but, nonetheless, educational values did not score highly. My limited practical research has indicated much the same thing. Headteachers hold beliefs and values, obviously, but they are not as transparent as one might expect. This implies that they are probably not conveyed clearly and powerfully within the school organisation. Successful transformational change will require that to be amended.

Beliefs and values can be communicated by

- ensuring that communications to staff say 'why' as well as 'what'

- repeating them *regularly* in staff briefings, as the reasons behind action points

- displaying short, succinct statements of Moral Purpose in the staff room

- insisting that beliefs and values form a major part of professional development agendas

- requiring departments to report formally on how beliefs and values influence their work and planning

- telling stories about the school that positively illustrate beliefs and values.

It is helpful to consider why a leader became a leader. One headteacher I spoke to said he 'just was in the right place at the right time' but could not recall any deep Moral Purpose either then or since. That is rare. Most heads with whom I have worked recall bright eyed days when they were full of Moral Purpose. They did not call it that, but that is what it was. They called it 'wanting to make a difference' which is, more or less, what Fullan said. It is a powerful thing.

Having personal Moral Purpose is energising, stimulating, rewarding and empowering but transformational leaders devise ways to transmit it to others. A vision without associated Moral Purpose will be limited in its impact: Moral Purpose will give it life, vitality, endurance and energy.

General Eisenhower exercised distinguished leadership in a totally different field to education yet the principle remained true in his area too

To be a leader a person must have followers, and to have followers a person must have their confidence. Hence the supreme quality of a leader is unquestionably integrity. The first great need is integrity and high purpose.

Characteristics of a leader

People do not follow others by accident. They follow those whose leadership they respect. It helps if the leader is liked, but respect is possible even when that is not the case. In *The 21 Irrefutable Laws of Leadership* (1998) John Maxwell argues that

> When people respect someone as a person – they admire her
>
> When people respect someone as a friend – they love her
>
> When people respect someone as a leader – they follow her.

Transformational leaders almost always **have the respect of those they are seeking to lead**. Respect is not gained without evidence. People willing to run through fire need to be sure that the person they are running for, and with, is worth it. Such respect is based on behaviour and attitude, on example and commitment.

Lee Iacocca delivered Chrysler from crisis through the power of outstanding leadership, much of it built on this principle: *Leadership means setting an example. When you find yourself in a position of leadership, people follow your every move.*

Good example is the foundation stone on which respect is built. Iacocca practised what he preached. At the time of financial crisis in his company, he reduced his salary to one dollar a year; that was 1979. In 1982 Chrysler generated the best profit in its history. Transformational change indeed.

Part of setting a good example is being **prepared to make sacrifices** in pursuit of the goal you talk about. People respect and follow leaders once they are convinced that what is set out as the vision is not 'all talk'. In Iacocca's case the evidence was plain. Maxwell illustrates it thus:

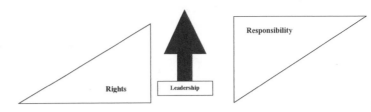

The more seriously you take your responsibility, the more likely you are to be to be prepared to l aside your rights.

Leaders who transform their world are **generous of spirit**, giving of themselves, their time, acknowledgement, encouragement and support. They are generous with praise. Mark Twain put it this way

> Great things happen when you don't care who gets the credit.

Transformational leaders have calculated that change of any magnitude cannot happen with individual endeavour alone; they seek to **develop teamwork and team commitment**. The change is more important than the individuals in the team making it. Leaders with magnanimity of spirit are likely to be leaders of successful teams, not least because team members quickly sense when leaders are in an endeavour for vain self-interest and are not all that committed.

Single-mindedness marks out the significant leader. It is not that they have no other interest, merely that the ambition to transform dominates much of their thinking. This single-mindedness means focusing on issues that are fundamental to the change process. In a recent survey I conducted as part of my work, a team of headteachers identified 20 characteristics of their job: of those 20 only five had anything directly to do with vision, standards or rewards which, according to Hay McBer, are the central emphases in successful organisations. Single-minded people, intent on transformation, prioritise those issues likely to produce significant change. Maxwell puts it like this

> If you focus your attention on the activities which rank in the top 20% in terms of importance, you will have an 80% return on your effort.

Single-mindedness leads to **determination**. Sometimes it is a lonely and painful road. Mahatma Gandhi explained

> To put up with misrepresentation and to stick to one's guns – come what may – this is the essence of leadership.

Gandhi and guns do not sit well together, but his principle is how it often has to be for leaders intent on making the transformational changes in their own world.

Great leaders give people space to make mistakes. They **develop a risk taking culture**, strong in the view that only by adventuring are new discoveries made. When Ofsted first began its work, teachers were frightened by the process and afraid to make mistakes. Many played safe and became vulnerable to criticism as dull, uninspirational and boring. As time has gone by the fear has diminished and teachers go for it, so that lessons appear more challenging. Headteachers can create a climate of freedom to experiment in search of the best. They trust colleagues and receive the rewards for such trust. Some graffiti summed up the dilemma

> If you TRUST students they let you down
>
> If you do NOT TRUST students they do you down.

It is very much like that with staff. Transformational leaders create a climate where it is safe to go for it, where the sting of fear has been drawn and where risk-taking is expected. Occasionally they get let down but, more often, they reap rich dividends.

When he was Chief Education Officer in Birmingham Tim Brighouse outlined five qualities of a good leader in 2000. Such leaders are

- infectiously optimistic
- good listeners
- committed
- takers of blame
- celebrators of others.

Howard Gardner, famed for his work on multiple intelligences, raised the issue of leadership in Regis College, USA, in 2003

> After spending most of my life studying intelligence, I agree with Ralph Waldo Emerson, that character in more important than intelligence.

That is clearly what the transformational leader needs and it could be argued that character is a combination of characteristics – good characteristics lead to good character.

General Norman Schwarzkopf shared Gardner's view:

> Leadership is a potent combination of strategy and character. But if you must be without one, be without strategy.

Transformational leaders want both.

Developing these skills and characteristics is a matter of slow learning. Many headteachers are working extraordinarily hard and could well do with following the maxim 'instead of... not... as well as': in most cases, the ability to introduce transformational change is going to depend on more learning rather than more effort as the diagram opposite illustrates.

Headteachers who are 'lead learners'

- read widely from leadership theory, both in education and in the wider world beyond

- visit other institutions ready to imbibe constructive ideas for advancement

- identify areas of relative weakness and seek out those whose advice can transform weakness to strength

- create a school culture where pursuit of excellence encourages the understanding that all need to continue to learn

- attend high quality training events (regardless of the cost), prepared to implement new ideas, after consideration, without guarantees of inevitable success.

If leadership ability can be learned and developed, it is worth spending the time to learn how to encourage that growth. The assumption that most heads are as good as they are going to get is misleading and defeatist: transformational headteachers are **lead learners**.

Irene Dalton in *Headlines*, the magazine of the Secondary Heads' Association, wrote (2003)

> The new jargon is about the 'transformational leader'. Unfortunately the context does not say transformation into what. Most headteachers will look back on years of transformation – the child for whom learning suddenly clicked; the school with low expectations and an 'it'll do' attitude transformed into a lively caring place with high expectations for all; the weak department changed

dramatically by the appointment of a new subject leader. But I fear that, now, the word transformation is another attempt to disguise change for the sake of it.

I hope she is wrong. Transformational change has been happening ever since time began, but the emphasis now encourages the broadening of those change experiences to embrace more and more institutions. It is absolutely right to note that changes have occurred, but that does not mean they have done so as much as they should nor could. Headteachers certainly need to ensure that they are not involved in 'change for change's sake'. Unless the chances are that there will be significant change for the better, best leave well alone. Perhaps leaders should devise a 'risk analysis' programme before attempting change: such a programme would identify potential areas of concern for staff, such as

- complicated initiatives for which careful communication may be needed

- pockets of resistance that threaten progress

- demands on staff and leaders that have a price attached to them

It needs to be remembered that not making a change can have significant associated risks too.

Ram Charan held strong views about the significance of leadership (2002):

> The culture of a school is the behaviour of its leaders. Leaders get the behaviour they exhibit and tolerate. You change the culture of a school by changing the behaviour of its leaders. You measure the change in culture by measuring the change in the personal behaviour of its leaders as well as the performance of the school.

Leaders are important. They make the transformational change. In Charan's world of business such change was needed. It is in education too.

In his best-seller, *The Road to Nab End*, William Woodruff (1999) describes life in Blackburn at the time of the first world war. He recalls the work of Mr Smalley, whom he called t'knocker up man,

> He came with his wire-tipped pole in the dark, six mornings a week, to shake our window until father stirred and shouted loud enough to be heard in the street below, 'We're up!'

Not every school is *up yet*, or not all have shouted loud enough for the government to hear. The rattle of the LIG money might awaken some but transformational leaders have already shouted 'We're up!' They are ready to go to work.

Chapter 2

Change is needed

We are all prisoners of our past. It is hard to think of things except in ways we have always thought of them. But that solves no problems and seldom changes anything.
Charles Handy

Charles Handy is right: it is hard, but it is not impossible. Change has been the managerial and business mantra of the nineties but it has always been like that. Already in 1806 Hegel observed that we '*stand at the gates of an important epoch, a time of ferment*'. It will always be so and so it should be. Stoll, Fink and Earl (2003) relate a telling story about a Parents' Evening at a school during which a parent complained that things were not like they used to be when she was at school. 'Why isn't it more like the way I was taught in school? It worked fine for me.' In a moment of inspired brilliance the teacher replied,

> I have a choice. I can either prepare your daughter for your past or for her future. Which would you prefer?

Change needs to happen in most organisations to prepare better for the world to come: we ought not to want to live in the past. The secret is to retain the best of the past while moving on with changes that will lead to a brighter tomorrow.

Who says change is needed?
Each generation only has chance to make its impact once and most human beings have a desire to do something significant with their lives. Often that will mean change. It is pleasant in the comfort zone but, for many leaders, personal fulfilment and satisfaction come from a sense of having made a difference: to do so almost always precludes settling in that comfort zone.

Most of us with spirit want to be part of successful beneficial change.

The government also takes a keen interest in change, particularly the pace of it. Michael Barber set the scene in an address to a conference of leading headteachers in 2002. He gave these reasons why change is necessary in education now

- Performance management is not changing things fast enough

- There is insufficient belief in excellence

- Reforms have been too clumsy and bureaucratic

- Knowledge is not created, distilled or transferred fast enough.

It is not that there is insufficient belief in excellence but rather insufficient understanding of what excellence is. Working with headteachers has convinced me that there is insufficient understanding of what excellence might look like, both for individual students and a whole school. It is difficult to define what 'excellent' would be, both in personal practice and in institutional life, because the present performance is often thought to be excellent: many headteachers are conscientious enough to try to be better if they know how to be. Searchers after excellence will:

- examine achievements of others and analyse them before deciding what lessons may be applied in one's own organisation

- create time and opportunity to think beyond one's present experience to determine what lies beyond it: this is often best achieved with others seeking similar objectives

- ask those with whom one works what might be done better: once that is understood it may well be easier to see the way ahead.

This whole process was developed much further in *Heading Towards Excellence* Rowling (2002).

Barber argues that in times past, the educational system has been prescriptive and that now, with the new knowledge that schools and leaders have, they are in a position to take responsibility for changing their schools with new opportunities and freedoms offered to them. Certainly there is a link to the standards agenda but why should there not be? Though headteachers would like some other measures than league tables to define achievement, still most of them seem prepared to accept that raising standards as measured by league tables is a vitally important issue. Transformational leadership throughout an organisation will expect to make a difference.

Michael Fullan (2002) noted that

> Deep and sustained change depends on the many of us, not just on the very few destined to be extraordinary.

Most of us will never be acknowledged in the wider world as extraordinary; but we will still make a great difference in the lives of many individuals, both students and colleagues. The transformational leader will enable her team to feel and enjoy that sense of fulfilment that comes from implementing change that makes a difference.

Why bother with change?
This concept of making a difference relates to the Moral Purpose foundation laid earlier: it is fundamental and without it neither leaders nor followers will have the heart, determination or aspiration to make change. Guiliani, in his book *Leadership* (2002), mentions his best friend Terry Hatton who died during the September 11 atrocity. Hatton was a distinguished member of the Fire Service. It fell to Guiliani to empty the locker of his friend, and, when he did so, he discovered a picture on its inside of

Terry Hatton carrying a child from flames to safety. That exemplifies Moral Purpose. Presumably, Hatton had that photograph there to remind him that for some people he was doing a job that meant the difference between life and death. It is a powerful energiser and motivator. It speaks of our reason for being. Too rarely do teachers reflect on what they are doing, not about schemes of work or assessment, but about making the difference to the lives of young people. We could do with a picture or two in our locker. Maybe that would provide the incentive to change in whatever ways we can to be even better at making the difference.

Alfred Nobel was an outstandingly successful businessman. He had made a vast fortune from the manufacture of explosives and armaments and his future seemed secure and bright when his brother died. A journalist in Paris made the mistake of confusing his brother with Alfred and wrote an obituary about Alfred not Frederick. A friend sent a copy of that obituary to Alfred Nobel. Amongst other more positive comments, it described him as a man who had made his fortune as 'a merchant of death'. It shook Nobel to his core. He decided that it was not enough to be 'successful' but that he wanted to do something with 'significance'. We know he did. He invested huge sums of money in the Nobel Prizes for Peace and Literature.

Transformational change is about moving from where we are to some place that has

- greater impact
- greater significance
- increased potential for making a difference.

That is why none of us, however successful, should stop thinking about the benefit of change. The aspiration to transformational change is admirable but making it happen is not easy.

Why change fails
When change fails is it because of:

- writing a memo instead of lighting a fire
- talking too much and saying too little
- declaring victory before the war is over
- looking for villains in all the wrong places

John Kotter outlines these four reasons why, for all the good intentions, change often does not result in the transformation envisaged. Transformational leadership is about lighting fires: too often one temptation is to think that because a concept is uppermost in your mind it must also be in someone else's. This is a serious mistake. Kotter argues that most leaders under-communicate their vision by a factor of ten. That does not mean that they have to say ten times as much – rather that they have to devise better ways to inspire and ignite the vision of those with whom they hope to see significant change. It is interesting that Fullan's Moral Purpose includes such strongly emotional words as 'passionate' and 'intense commitment'. These are words with fire in them. They are not going to be achieved by memos alone, no matter how well they are written. The transformational leader will devise ways to ensure that enough fires are kindled.

The Beacon School initiative offered a glorious opportunity to light fires. Schools used a variety of strategies in pursuit of Beacon goals but ours was undoubtedly and unashamedly about kindling ambition and life in partner institutions alongside new fires kindling in our own school. The sticks were the pleasures afforded in seeing students responding to their own achievement, demonstrated through stories and slides about the issuing of results on examination results day. One of the great motivators throughout the dark days of winter is the thought of student and family celebration on results day that we have all worked in partnership to achieve.

The larger sticks were the shared practice on monitoring and gender related strategies. These led to significant transformation in all our partner schools as well as in our own, resulting in over 10% increases on GCSE performance in one year in three schools. Once a fire has been lit, it is easier to prepare another.

Lighting fires is an art. You can use modern artificial devices and save much time and effort, but there is something satisfying about laying a coal fire that quickly takes a hold. Some small sticks first, because they catch easily, then some larger ones that, though slower, will establish the fire well, and finally the coal itself. Some staff grasp the vision with little apparent effort or persuasion, others take longer but are vital to the establishment of sustainable life. Lighting transformational fires is an art too.

Leaders get where they are partly because they are good talkers: being able to articulate your thinking is a precious gift. However, it invites the dangers of

- talking too much and saying too little

- thinking that what you say others hear

- believing that everybody is as good with words

- neglecting the learning preferences of other people.

The acid test is how much people can remember, or demonstrate behaviour that is affected by, what is said. Transformational change requires a shrewd assessment of what to say, how much to say and how to say it.

The feel-good factor in an organisation is important. Kotter argues that declaring victory before the war is over can have a seriously detrimental effect.

In any change effort there is a need to be seen to be getting somewhere because it

> refreshes spirits
> renews commitment
> energises those involved
> ignites some of the reticent.

There are Short Term Wins discussed later, yet premature celebration can leave an organisation vulnerable to conflict. It is all very well to have short-term celebrations, but extravagant claims are not helpful in pursuit of transformational change. Arsene Wenger, brilliant manager at Arsenal Football Club, declared in mid-season that he thought it likely that his excellent team could go all season without losing a game. They had been astonishingly good but in May 2003 when they were overtaken in the finishing straight by Manchester United, the celebration was seen to have been premature. Kotter was right.

In meetings of headteachers, middle managers have a hard time! It seems from my experience that they are thought to be the principle reason why certain schools are not brilliantly successful. As Professor Reynolds declared: (June 2001) '*I would like the government to move beyond its unhealthy obsession with headteachers and focus on middle management. Most heads are now as good as they are going to get, whereas middle management is usually inadequate.*'

That contrasts with Kotter's argument that change is likely to fail if we look for villains in the wrong places. Lest he be misunderstood, he amplified this as follows

> The perception that large organisations (schools) are filled with recalcitrant middle mangers who resist all change is not only unfair, it is untrue.

Middle managers are an easy target: doubtless some are poor, but so are some headteachers. Charan explained his view that leaders get what they are prepared to tolerate. Transformational leaders will expect to address the inadequacies of middle managers by one means or another. Removing weak middle managers has been no easier than removing weak headteachers, though the first, second and third instinct of advanced transformational leaders is to exercise transformation with these people too, where possible. When it is not, something drastic has to be done and this will require creativity and skill. Government initiatives like the Leadership Incentive Grant are new opportunities to engage in creative and constructive means of unblocking the impediments to progress. My experience indicates that middle managers in this situation are as aware of their problem as the leader is, but are naturally and instinctively defensive. I would be myself. It is no good headteachers expecting middle managers to fall on their swords when it is rare that heads do. Dealing with middle management in a way that releases and energises both them and the organisation is as big a challenge as one could wish for.

Transformational change has to be all about people. In Kotter's words

> The central issue is never strategy, structure, culture or systems. All those elements, and others, are important. But the core of the matter is always about changing the behaviour of people, and behaviour change happens in highly successful situations mostly by speaking to people's feelings.

I have heard it argued that

I CAN is greater than I Q

But I believe there is a more significant truth than that

I WANT TO is greater than I CAN.

Influencing people by the ethos you create, the empathy you display, the interest you show, the support you give and the inspiration you bring is likely to create a desire to want to which is far more powerful than I Q. Transformational leaders have this two pronged approach

- to skill people to the point where they believe they CAN

- to inspire people to feel that they WANT TO.

This is not easy work. Applying off-the-shelf ideas leaders can make some successful change in organisations, but adopting a more fundamental approach will create the momentum in an organisation that will lead to transformation and sustainability.

It is a relatively recent change in thinking. The traditional pattern has been

ANALYSE → THINK → CHANGE

This is valid and has stood the test of time. It is not to be discarded but adding an overlay gives it more power.

SENSE → FEEL → CHANGE

People are not the same. I have found that some of the thinkers are highly sceptical about all the recent talk about emotional intelligence: but it seems so sensible, so true to life, so logical and realistic. People who feel in their heart what they are convinced of in their head are going to be more effective than those whose approach is one *or* the other.

Generally, people travel along the Emotional Comfort Highway: this is where they feel at ease with how they feel, emotions are well under control, their feelings exercise some influence but do not dominate. The power to change and influence is less significant when people travel in this area than when they are coaxed or coerced out of it by the appeal of a proposal or the fear of a threat.

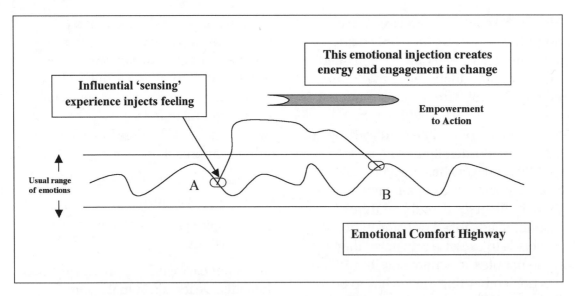

The attraction of a proposal at point A in life appeals to the senses: it may be the perceived need of a troubled teenager for which you have the answer, or the possibility of achieving outstanding success with a group of students; it may be the thought of pleasing someone for whom you have great admiration. But always it will be something that goes beyond the cerebral into the heart. This touching of the senses often results in the 'feeling' that I want to be engaged with it: this in turn can lead to significant energy and engagement in the process of making transformational change.

The emotional engagement may fade, as at point B, but fresh impetus can be given to it by added attractions.

The same process can be triggered by an injection of threat or danger: should this happen at A, the curve would move downwards out of the Emotional Comfort Highway. Energy is generated by negative emotions too. This is most obvious when a school is threatened with closure: sensing all that this will mean, the staff, and parents with students, often engage in a frantic, determined and passionate struggle to survive and succeed. A wise leader uses such 'negative' appeals to the senses with discretion, because, though the effects can be dramatic, startling people

into action in the short term by a short, sharp shock is uncomfortable and the energy generated by threat or fear is not sustainable for very long.

Even before they are analysed some 'facts' and their perceived implications are enough to stir some people into action, whether it is SATs scores or places in league tables. Transformational change can follow from that approach.

However, leaders who are seeking to connect with the emotions of staff calculate how best to demonstrate issues that connect with sensitivity. It may be showing a picture, telling a story or portraying a scene. Whatever it is, it needs to connect with the deeper being, the emotional core, of staff, and from it there emerges energised activity that makes the difference. The two approaches are not mutually exclusive: transformational leaders will be aware of the potential of both.

Change does involve emotion, this much is clear.

The **POSITIVE** feelings generated by change			The **NEGATIVE** feelings generated by change	
faith	confidence		fear	anger
well-being	trust	v	insecurity	worry
pleasure	optimism		pessimism	gloom
pride	passion		pride	panic
excitement	hope		excitement	despair

The Sense-Feel-Change approach will recognise that all the emotions involved are not easily analysed or fully understood. But they are real. They are people's perceptions and so they are their reality. Transformational leaders evaluate the impact that negative emotions have in the workforce, impeding the change effort, and address them through sensitively exposing them in an attempt to move them. Positive emotions must be a source of renewal and strength in those who feel them. Achieving this is skilled work requiring considerable emotional intelligence in the leader but I believe that emotional intelligence can be learned, developed over time. There is hope for us all.

Resistance to change

It still feels more respectable in this country to object to change on the grounds of one's rational argument than on feeling; that does not mean, however, that feeling is less valid. Four objections to change are common, each rooted in both emotion and logic

- There has been too much change already

- We are far too busy to take on anything more

- A few more quick fixes and all will be well

- We are doing well, what is the hurry?

A good argument can be made for each objection, and there is usually someone who will articulate it. Stereotypically, they are the well-established people who have a 'power base to protect'. They talk about valid issues like workload, rights, exploitation, whiz kids and pressure. They generate high emotion and play on the fears of others. They rarely have an alternative strategy to stalling change efforts: theirs is an effort to arrest the development of an idea's momentum. Sometimes they safeguard a school from

disastrous initiatives mostly they inhibit genuine much-needed transformation.

Some resistance is head-on, easily seen coming. Other opposition to change is more subtle; quite difficult to isolate because it is covert. Some appeals are to higher moral purposes, a challenge indeed: some to the incompetence of those trying to make the changes. Almost always there is much more to all this than merely rational arguments. Discerning and understanding the emotional complexities goes some way to addressing the resistance.

There are four tensions surrounding change

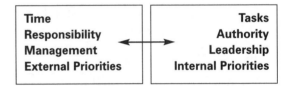

People understand what is demanded in transformational change but argue that, though it is good, there is no time to do it. One hears 'No time' so often. It is genuine enough and needs to be treated seriously. Transformational leaders learn how to create time, sometimes by shrewd management of funds to employ new staff, sometimes by reducing work practices that are not a priority, sometimes by setting aside other demands.

Within all transformation there is opportunity for staff to grow and develop. Tension arises when responsibility is given but authority is withheld. Transformational leaders release people's creativity and energy by giving responsibility and trusting with authority. This is safeguarded by the Opportunity Triangle:

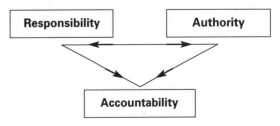

Good leadership gives people responsibility, allows autonomy and unashamedly calls to account. This should not be heavy-handed but it should be clearly understood. According to research, one of the significant differences between the worlds of business and education is that leaders in education are less good at calling people to account. It is difficult to know why that should be. Accountability can be a liberating, enriching, enabling and energising force, if handled wisely, but it will only be successful if it is accompanied by the delegation of genuine responsibility and authority.

Koestenbaum (2002) introduced a formula illustrating the ingredients that enable empowerment (E)

$$E = A * D * S$$

where A is autonomy granted by the leader to the team member, D is the direction given and S is the support offered. Koestenbaum makes the point that should any one of the three variables be zero then the empowerment also is zero. Giving autonomy is obviously crucial.

There has been debate about the relative merits of setting as opposed to mixed ability teaching. The Opportunity Triangle is useful here. If responsibility for performance is delegated to a middle manager, with the accompanying authority to use whatever grouping mechanisms she thinks best, accountability is going to judge outcomes and not meddle. Transformational leaders may be tempted to interfere and not truly release people in partnership. This is stifling and will prove counter-productive.

There can be real tensions between management and leadership. The leaders have the bright ideas, the managers see it as their role to 'stop them going too far'. Indeed managers do

have such a role but the tension can become insufferable: 'nothing is possible', it 'cannot be afforded', money needs to 'be saved for a rainy day', risks need to be avoided, finance should be spent on other things. The 'facts on the table' may support the safety first approach. The first time I proposed spending over £20 000 on a staff training conference, more than one person suggested the money could be better spent. How can it be easily argued that the benefits of all staff being together, working on whole staff development and transformational issues, is more valuable than money spent on books? I am sure it is, but it is difficult to prove it to managers who are not leaders.

Perhaps the greatest of all tensions is between imposed *external* expectations and *internal* transformational aspirations that seek to address recognised priorities in the local setting. It is a pressure leaders could do without. The Department for Education and Skills is also working to a transformational agenda but this can make it more difficult for those working transformationally in the local setting. There is no simple solution to the problem.

There are two strategies that are helpful in conflict

Don't fight if you can't win	Don't rush to defend yourself

It would be pleasant if no one ever disagreed – or would it? It would be boring, probably, and stifling of creativity. Some of the world's greatest inventions happened as a result of battle! However, a leader who engages in dispute that she has no chance of winning can set back the cause of transformation for a long time.

As many people's first instinct is to be negative, it is foolish to defend your corner at the slightest sign of opposition. It is not easy to keep quiet but it is necessary. Recently, I shared a brilliant transformational idea I had worked out with a committee that had been called together to introduce the proposal. There was no problem, because I did most of the talking. A second meeting was called to discuss the matter. The first ten minutes were about what a bad idea it was and how it would not work. Though tempted to argue, I didn't. I just watched how the climate changed as people were given space to thrash it out. If we rush to defend things people are bound to challenge, if only to watch the reaction. The quickest way to draw a crowd of young people together in my school is if someone shouts 'Fight! Fight!' The whole world gathers to see a fight.

What needs changing anyway?

Psychologist Eric Hoffer said

> In times of change the learners will inherit the earth, while the knowers will find themselves beautifully equipped to deal with a world that no longer exists.

Change is either going to happen to us, or, better, be created by us. No self-respecting leader wants to be left washed up on the beach hoping to catch some future wave. Far wiser to think like John Schaar

> The future is not some place we are going but one we are creating. The paths to it are not found but made, the activity of making them changes both the maker and the user.

The current emphasis is on 'changing the culture'. Culture is defined by Morgan (1997) as 'how organisations work when no-one is watching'. It is an appropriate emphasis. Fullan (1992) believes that 'any attempt to improve a school without addressing the culture is doomed to be tinkering' because school culture influences readiness for change.

The obvious questions about changing the culture of a school are

- From what to what?

- How will this change the behaviour of people in the school?

David Hopkins (2002) said that the cultural changes he expected to see centred on

Teaching	*Learning*
Moral Purpose	*Innovation*

- Hopkins argues that transformation of teaching will require a new look at teaching strategies which give the '*curriculum its power*'.

- The challenge for learning is to '*integrate prior and new knowledge, to solve problems individually and in groups and accept that learning involves struggle*'.

- Fullan's Moral Purpose appears again, defined by Hopkins as '*raising the standard – closing the gap*'. There is justifiable national concern about the disproportionate difference in achievement between those from diverse backgrounds and also about '*in-school variation*', the issue that some departments do well yet other fare badly – in the same school.

- Perhaps following Jim Collins, Hopkins sees innovation as an opportunity to change towards excellence. '*Innovation*,' he said, '*Is a process not an event, about moving from good practice to best practice, replication and scale up.*'

In schools, transformational change is being attempted in order to change the culture (see illustration on page 26).

A change in the culture of organisations is being attempted in many schools in these seven areas and others. In order to achieve the transformation it will need distributed leadership. Alma Harris of Warwick University (2003) outlined three requirements for change

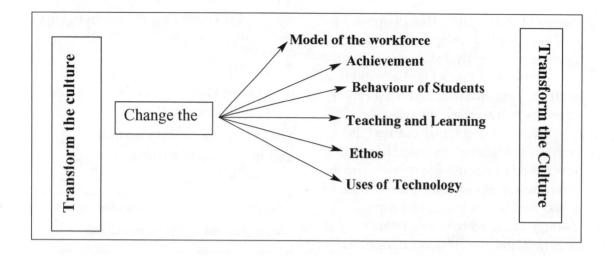

- Maximising the potential of existing leadership

- Widening the opportunity to include teachers more

- Creating meaningful professional development to enable teachers to develop leadership potential.

The necessity for change will need constant emphasis. Jack Welch found that '*You've got to talk about change every second of the day.*' I would not go quite that far, but it certainly worked for him. And no half measures will do if transformation is to happen.

Leadership is important; change is certainly both expected and needed. Seven steps to transformation will be examined in the chapters following. Any successful transformation will have gone through these seven stages, in the order shown. Though some may merge from time to time the phases are distinct and different. Some take longer than others but all have their place.

Chapter 3

Feel the Need

Our emotions have a mind of their own, one which can hold views quite independently of our rational mind.
Daniel Goleman

Sir John Harvey-Jones knew a great deal about transformational leadership;

> It is impossible to change organisations not accepting the danger of their present way of doing things... organisations only change when the people in them change, and people will only change when they accept in their hearts that change must occur.

There is little real danger for schools. The nearest education came to being endangered was in the era of naming and shaming. There are perceived to be some difficult questions to answer if a school is well down the league tables or not performing well on value added tables, but it is hardly the danger faced by companies such as Harvey-Jones ran, where the stakes were very high indeed. If change is to happen it has to be much more pushed by desire than in flight from danger, but that should not make motivation any the less.

The possibility of losing grants or being interrogated by officials from the DfES about the school's performance may become dangers in the future. The publication of the performance of schools and particularly of individual staff would be intimidating. It would be strongly resisted and may never happen, but it would certainly be perceived as dangerous. How sad if schools only performed better if they were subject to the actions they so oppose. Schools need to be ambitious for transformation themselves, not wait until pressure is applied to make them become better.

Interestingly Harvey-Jones spoke about emotional involvement long before it was articulated as it is now. Accepting the need for change '*in their hearts*' confirms that full emotional engagement is necessary before transformational change begins.

Larry Bossidy, one time CEO of Allied Signal, used the metaphor of 'burning platforms'.

> The leader's job is to help everyone see that the platform is burning, whether the flames are apparent or not. The process of change begins when people decide to take the flames seriously and manage in view of the facts, and that means a brutal understanding of reality. You need to know what the reality is so that you know what needs changing.

This is not the language of the English educational world, indeed it is almost anathema to it, but academic researchers into transformation regard it is as fundamental. John Kotter expands on the theme:

> By far the biggest mistake people make when trying to change organisations is to plunge ahead without establishing a high enough **sense of urgency** in fellow managers and employees.

Jim Collins, in *Good to Great* (2001), agrees;

> Those companies that became great displayed two distinctive forms of disciplined thought. The first was that they infused their entire process with the brutal facts of reality, the second that they developed a simple, yet deeply insightful, frame of reference for all decisions.

He called them '*brutal facts*'. Brutal is an unexpected adjective to choose to go with facts; such facts sounds painful to acknowledge; one can only imagine that they create the sort of sense of urgency that Kotter believed was so important. Unfortunately this is not a once-in-a lifetime experience. Collins' research team went on,

> Unlike comparison companies, the good to great companies continually refined the path to greatness with the brutal facts.

It may not be pleasant, it may not be painless, but it is certainly consistent and it is evidently successful. These brutal facts in education may be linked to the despised tables or to attendance statistics or to the poor development of new technology in school or to the toxicity in the staffroom: indeed, on occasions, some brutal facts may be explicitly spelled out by Ofsted. There are a multitude of issues but, in my experience, schools seem less inclined than the world of business to confront them: perhaps it is because business has to or it dies. Schools are able to survive for quite a while even when they are very sick, though they do so at considerable cost to students and communities.

Complacency Kills Urgency	Reasons for Complacency	• past success • lack of visible crisis • low standards • little competion • insufficient feedback from outsiders

Complacency kills urgency. Research evidence indicates that urgency is important so complacency is more deadly than it appears.

Signs of Complacency:

- **Acceptance that what is being done is a good as it gets**

- **Few new creative ideas; regular use of same processes, lesson plans**

- **Little questioning of practice**

- **Ridicule by staff of new initiatives**

- **Low emphasis on training and development**

- **Lack of interest in the success of others**

- **Defence mechanisms go up quickly when raising standards is talked about**

- **Few visits to other institutions or to attend developmental courses**

- **Easy acceptance of, and excuses made to justify, poor performance**

- **No sharp challenges to low results**

- **Comparative statistics glossed over or dismissed as unimportant**

- **Constant referral to environmental or socio-disadvantage factors**

- **Most promotions internal**

Schools can live in the past. I remember wondering about the school that for years called itself by its current name but wrote underneath 'formerly X Grammar School'. What any of us were formerly may be an enemy of the future, but only if it becomes a source of complacency: what any school was ten years ago is of little consequence to today's students.

- **Is my school complacent, with no sense of urgency?**

- **What are the signs?**

- **What might be done about it?**

Very few crises appear absolutely without warning but there are schools where, because the brutal facts are not sought and confronted, the staff continue working in the belief that all is well. Clearly no transformational change will happen here. The facts are there to be unearthed but some leaders opt for denial. This kills urgency.

At one time it seemed that nearly every Ofsted report included the comment 'not enough challenge'; it is not easy to evaluate exactly what students should achieve and such comments were often dismissed as easy talk. Teachers often said, 'We are not dealing with chemicals or inanimate materials that are predictable'. This is true but it is not an excuse to conceal poor performance. The government has expressed concern about some apparently high achieving schools because it has cause to believe their standards, and their expectations, are too low. They consider them 'coasting', sometimes 'complacent'; either way urgency is lacking.

Competition has become an unacceptable word in education. It is a pity because, though collaboration has much to commend it, so does a healthy dose of local competition. It is problematic when competition does not take place on an even playing field but at its best local competition, as opposed to monopoly of provision, can challenge complacency.

Schools are autonomous units and can live in splendid isolation if they wish. Little feedback from parents, scant regard for LEA input, no meaningful contact with anyone to disturb the status quo; not exactly what Michael Barber (2002) had in mind when he challenged schools to consider the work of the best, in and outside education, to sharpen practice and promote transformation. Complacency kills all that.

John Kotter wisely remarked,

> Never underestimate the magnitude of the forces that reinforce complacency and that help to maintain the *status quo*.

The excuses schools use to sustain inertia are predictable:

All schools have these problems

Even if they do, it does not mean that your school should; at least not until all the hard facts have been put on the table, analysed and evaluated.

You can't make a silk purse out of sow's ear

If any statement typifies low standards, that is it. Not only is it demeaning and insulting but it kills all sense of urgency.

It's not us, it's them

Applied across the board, this sort of statement precludes taking any action for change. The head can say it about the staff, the middle managers about the Senior Leadership Team, the staff about the students, the students about the staff. Say it and believe it, and you can wave goodbye to transformational change.

There is nothing we can do about it

Occasionally there is nothing that can be done, but usually there is. If one exposes the brutal facts, opening up honest debate and dialogue and is willing to explore a situation, all manner of possibilities emerge.

Jack Welch saw Superficial Congeniality as an equally big challenge

Superficial congeniality: a situation where people are pleasant on the surface, with distrust and savagery rumbling beneath it.

Superficial Congeniality is damaging is energy sapping is demoralising

These are nine actions that are useful in challenging the characteristic ways of resisting (see table below).

a) Expose the brutal facts

John Kotter observed that people '*get used to stepping over the body in the living room*'. The facts need to be exposed, the facts to do with data and those to do with emotion. In order to change behaviour, people need first to know precisely where they are. Motivation is not a thinking word – it is a feeling word. Exposing the brutal facts will generate understanding and emotion. That should not be avoided.

Expose brutal facts	Stop happy talk	Reveal other comparable situations where higher targets are reached
Don't allow people to consider only their own results	Illustrate what a difference better performance would make	Use simpler, clearer, and better data
Show people what they stand to gain	Reveal the progress of competitors and the threat they pose	Put complaints on the table

b) Stop happy talk

Successes should not be denied but they should not be allowed to hide the reality revealed by the facts. Although happiness is a powerful emotional force, in the wrong place it can lead to denial, and damage the potential for transformation.

c) Reveal other comparable sources of data where higher targets are reached

Though every school is different some are similar enough to make comparison useful. Comparing performance data is helpful. Discovering that two schools in similar circumstances have vastly different exam results, attendance figures, truancy rates, extracurricular involvement or behaviour problems is worth further investigation, not merely to find an excuse, but to interrogate for transformation. Discovering that others with much the same profile as you are achieving so much more can generate considerable emotion and this emotion can be useful in transformation.

Earl and Katz (2002) point out that,

> Data do not provide right answers or quick fixes. Instead, they are necessary but not sufficient elements of the conversations that ensue.

d) Use simpler clearer and better data

'Lies, damned lies and statistics' says the old adage. There is plenty of data around but it is too complex for general consumption. It needs interpreting, simplifying and illustrating pictorially so that it is intelligible and indisputable. Statistics can be used to defend a position in order to avoid the brutal facts. It is a wasteful exercise.

e) Illustrate what a difference better performance would make

A sense of urgency is sometimes evoked when people realise that they are letting others down. That would have to be handled with care and set against the reality that unless there is transformational change in some situations, many people are being let down.

f) Don't allow people to consider only their own results

Most of us would have little sense of urgency if we lived in our own private world. Urgency springs out of a realisation that we may not be doing what we ought to be. Defensiveness, allied to articulacy, can make a substantial case over almost anything: to create that urgency is likely to require valid, fair comparisons outside of, and beyond, one's own organisation.

g) Show people what they stand to gain

People's motivation is often highest when linked to concern for others but is underpinned by a natural desire for personal fulfilment. A sense of urgency can be developed by raising awareness of how much more fulfilment there is in being actively and positively involved in team work towards a transformational goal.

h) Reveal the progress of competitors and the threat they pose

Collins speaks of *continual* refinement, implying that organisations progressing very well in transformational change may have, at any time, to face the challenges of reality all around. After a prolonged period with no near educational neighbours, either geographically or academically, a new City Academy arrived on our doorstep last year. What is more, the local council declared that it was supporting the development of the new school in order to recruit some students presently attending our school into theirs. This proposal aroused a justifiable sense of urgency which propelled us into increasing our attention to transformational change. Threats do indeed focus the mind.

i) Put complaints on the table.
It is tempting to deal with complaints by either defending them or by minimising them and their effect on colleagues. Both approaches have merits at times but in terms of creating a sense of urgency it can be really helpful to put complaints on the table so that it becomes transparently obvious that there is a problem. This applies particularly when there is a consistency about the issues at the centre of complaints indicating that a problem needs to be addressed.

Now let us think more about these brutal facts.

SCHOOL SNAPSHOT

THE SCHOOL Clifton Green Primary School (3-11), York
Headteacher: Sheila Audsley
Primary, with Nursery attached, Roll 370, Free School Meals 35%

THE STARTING POINT
Ofsted inspection revealed school in difficulties (March 2000)

Eleven issues raised, all relating to Leadership and Management

New headteacher appointed from September 2000

Relationships between leadership and staff damaged

Behaviour of children aggressive, unruly, generally poor

An amalgamation with a school with poor achievement pending

The headteacher had been asked by LEA to take over this school in difficulty and was designated to begin in September 2000

THE TRANSFORMATION SOUGHT
To improve the relationships between leadership and staff

To prepare the school for a successful amalgamation with a local Infant School

HELPING STAFF TO FEEL THE NEED
Using the Ofsted report I explained what was unsatisfactory in the school

I compared what was expected with what was being achieved

Staff were encouraged to discuss Ofsted's findings and to outline their frustrations with how things had become so bad

Staff were made aware that, working together, they were the only ones who could change this

We shared how wonderful it would be for our children if we did this together

An emphasis was put on how good they would feel if they achieved a breakthrough

I confirmed my faith in their ability to be successful and commended open and welcome responses from staff to new ideas for transformation

OUTCOMES
Best test results the school had ever had, 20% up at Key Stage 2 in 2002

90% of children achieved national average or higher at Key Stage 1

School Achievement Award 2001/2

Successful amalgamation, including huge increase in achievement amongst children who had been barely able to write their names

WAS IT WORTH IT?
Staff have a new sense of confidence in their ability to make transformational change and that makes it worth the effort

COMMENTS
'To make rapid improvement there has to be a whole school focus with full understanding and agreement with what is being done'

'Staff have to feel emotionally involved in the need for change and the change process'

SCHOOL SNAPSHOT

THE SCHOOL West Oaks School and Technology College, Leeds Headteacher: Hilary McEwan

All age special generic school, opened in 1991. Doubled in size in 10 years

Recently took over a school in serious weaknesses

145 children on two sites

The school has had two outstanding Ofsted reports and has Beacon status

THE STARTING POINT

There was need to adjust to new government requirements after 1998

THE TRANSFORMATION SOUGHT

The ability to offer a range of support and services to mainstream schools to promote inclusion and the retention of children in their own local primary schools

To transcend the sector and make ourselves a valuable commodity to our partner schools and communities

HELPING STAFF TO FEEL THE NEED

I outlined the trigger that would necessitate change

Encouraged staff to develop their own excellence which would 'strengthen, not diminish, us'

Proposed we would go for Beacon and Technology status which would strengthen our credibility further and stressed that 'if we don't change we wither and die'

OUTCOMES

Beacon and Technology status achieved alongside outstanding Ofsted reports

A consultancy wing has developed generating over £120 000 per year

WAS IT WORTH IT?

A real sense of mission and fulfilment amongst staff

Appreciation from partners of services available

Enormous benefit to young people

COMMENTS

Change processes have to be systematic, even then not all stakeholders will 'buy into' them

When we seek change again I will ' articulate more succinctly the change process and protocols'

We learned about change and used a process best summed up by Grayson and Hodges in Everybody's Business

Recognise the Trigger; Make a Case; Scope the Issues; Commit to Action; Integrate Strategies; Engage Stakeholders; Measure and report the Impact of Change

Chapter 4

Face the Facts

No one ever grew as a result of being measured.
Cockroft Report 1982

It is amazing how many interpretations there can be of facts. The leader's role is to know the facts and to analyse and interpret them accurately. Early impressions can be gained from some facts which create a sense of urgency – something must be done about this – but deeper, fuller analysis needs to be undertaken. Ultimately the leader needs to have all the facts on the table.

An increasing wealth of data is available pertaining to achievement. Before it can be decided whether the culture of achievement needs changing the facts have to be in the open. Emotional responses are entirely valid but they need to be supported by a clear grasp of the facts too.

Bossidy and Charan (2002), whose job it was to promote transforming change in GEC and later in their own corporations, discussed facts with the key leaders in their organisations. Their observations are interesting.

> When we ask leaders to describe their organisations' strengths and weaknesses, they generally state the strengths fairly well, but they are not so good at identifying weaknesses. And when we ask what they are going to do about the weaknesses, the answers are rarely clear or cohesive.

Strengths and Weaknesses
Finding the facts
Where are they?
How do you dig them out?
How are they interpreted?

Facing the facts

Who faces the facts?

What exposure are they given?

How do you deal with responses?

Where are they?

The facts about an organisation are everywhere. We are increasingly data rich about many issues: test scores, attendance and truancy figures, staff absence, exclusion rates, special needs and numbers of computers in school are all supported by hard evidence. Interpreters of data are available as well, ranging through Midyis and Yellis to Panda reports and Fischer Family Trust comparators. Local Education Authority data is now well-advanced and freely available at all key stages. This data is easy to assemble but is often interpreted by the leader, or the Senior Leadership Team and retained only by them: that is not facing the facts and is likely to have limited value.

There is a wealth, too, of softer evidence, such as the level of staff morale which although significant is not easy to measure. There are no league tables about staff morale. Wouldn't it be interesting to compare and contrast league tables of staff morale with those for examination performance? Equally, it is difficult to discover data about the level of motivation of staff or their relationship to the vision of the school. Some behaviour issues can be measured using hard evidence, but it is not so easy to establish the facts about underlying causes.

Some evidences of low morale are easy to measure: attendance rates exceeding 5% indicate a problem worth checking. If there are still many staff cars in the school car park after 5pm morale is almost certainly high. A mass exodus as soon as the bell goes is a sign of poor staff morale. Morale is a great energiser; it is odd that so little attention is paid to checking it out. What can be done about it?

> **Tell tale signs about Low Staff Morale**
>
> - high absence rate
> - few volunteers to serve on working groups
> - negative tone of conversations in staff room
> - rate at which car park vacates after school
> - energy levels: slow pace at which people move
> - little laughter in school
> - support given to other colleagues involved in initiatives
> - openness to proposals to improve practice
> - cynical staff control staff room

1. Make a senior colleague responsible for preparing a method of determining the level of staff morale

2. Introduce new ways of acknowledging staff contributions

3. Develop systems for finding out what is being done well and praise it both privately and openly

4. Spend money on providing high quality conditions in which staff may work in classrooms and the staff room

5. Leaders meet staff systematically, anually at least, to talk about how they feel about their work, noting their observations and attending to them

6. Plan social events as an acknowledgement of service from staff and make a point of greeting them personally to say 'thank you'

7. Make time to visit those who are engaged in after school activity to

thank them in front of those with whom they are working

8. Be at the school entrance directly after school to say goodnight to those who depart briskly!

How do you dig the facts out?
Some facts lie on the surface for all to see and evoke an emotional response ranging from great pleasure to despair. In secondary schools, this can be particularly noticeable at the time of publication of examination results. If results are shown for each department, those who have achieved highly are pleased to discuss it, while those whose results are less good feel some embarrassment. It is interesting to compare how different institutions publish results; some favour putting the facts on the table for all to see, others deal with them privately; some deal with them hardly at all.

When the data is beneath the surface, some mechanism has to be found to dig out the facts. As part of the Leadership Incentive Grant package, an Assessment Tool was introduced. Clearly the product of much thought, it offered schools a survey document with 41 sections to be used to ascertain the perceptions of staff on a wide range of key issues. This LIG exercise was introduced for all the staff in my school and provided useful 'brutal facts' to put on the table. For each of the 41 sections being considered, the leadership team noted where they believed the evidence was in the school that applied to the section under consideration. This was done so that staff could be reminded of systems and procedures in place in school in order for them to properly decide how well the school matched the criteria being assessed. Often snap judgements can be made without forethought. If the hard facts to emerge were going to be taken seriously it was necessary to ensure that all judgements were made on full information. It was interesting, but

Observation: The nearer a person is to the top of an organisation the higher will be her perception of the quality of the leadership.

To get the truth, you need to go down the organisation as well.

perhaps not surprising, to discover that the positive perceptions of matching criteria really well declined the further from the top of the organisation that was surveyed. The senior staff thought things were better than the staff lower down the hierarchy. This is likely to be the case in most organisations and a very good reason why the facts need to be open to more than just a few leaders at the head of an organisation. If we are serious about transformation, we need to find out the opinions of staff across the whole organisation. And they have to be exposed.

How are the facts interpreted?
Even with hard data it is not always easy to get agreement on what the evidence means. When talking of facing the facts, leaders should not put a spin on those facts. What is important is to establish which facts are going to be put on the table for wider consultation. Their interpretation should be a private matter at this stage, to prevent the initial response of defensiveness.

Who faces the facts?
Here is the big decision. Often only those directly involved with issues under concern are consulted in discussions on the brutal facts: that may be fine, but there is a sense in which the more people who are involved, the more likely it is that a transformational move will have broad support.

What exposure are the facts given?

Leaders sometimes convince themselves that the staff are not aware of what is going on – which may well be true. More often, however, they have worked out the implications of the brutal facts themselves so that opening them out is sensible. Interpretations of facts, as they are perceived, can lead to some unfortunate and dangerous misunderstandings: more transparent leaders will do things better.

How do you deal with responses?

It is regarded as risky to let people know the truth lest some member of staff take advantage. Leaders may be concerned that the facts reflect badly on them. The truth is that if the facts are not exposed openly, some version of them will be discussed privately. Goffee and Jones (2000) suggest that the best leaders *selectively show their weaknesses.* When the truth about the brutal facts is out, wise leaders who want to make transformational change seize the moment even if they are fearful. Most people appreciate openness and honesty and respond to it. Few people are comfortable working with those who never admit things are not all they ought to be. And leaders are meant to model the behaviour they seek in others. If the facts indeed appear brutal from a personal perspective, how I respond will reflect what I might expect when the same situation happens with my staff. There is a lot at stake.

Research conducted by the Stanford University team concluded that the companies progressing from good to great followed four procedures in regard to brutal facts. Once the facts are opened up to people's scrutiny,

a) Lead with questions not answers

The facts as they are understood are in the open. A private view may be held on what they mean, but Collins (2001) argues that the leaders of companies which

Lead with questions not answers

Engage in dialogue and debate, not coercion

Conduct autopsies without blame

Build in checking mechanisms where people can say what they feel

became great encouraged people to look at the facts with them, by asking questions not making statements. This sometimes feels like lost time but it is not.

The brutal facts may be that boys compared to girls in school X are underachieving by about 15%. The leader may have her explanation for this but would be wise not to offer it. Instead, she should put the facts on the table and ask questions.

This approach is wisest because

- the leader may have got it wrong

- others will think there is no point in making any suggestions since 'they' have it all decided anyway

- people who are to be a part of the transformation need to feel involved at the start.

Fred Purdoe, executive of Pitney Bowes, summed it up:

> When you turn over rocks and look at all the squiggly things underneath, you can either put the rock down, or you can say, ' My job is to turn over rocks and look at squiggly things', even if what you see scares the hell out of you.'

It is the transformational leader's job to look at the squiggly things and ask questions with others, not give answers.

The greatest leaders have practised this principle of establishing the brutal facts. During the war Churchill feared that his towering, charismatic personality might deter people from delivering bad news to him in its starkest form, so he created an entirely new department, the Statistical Office, with the principle function of feeding him the brutal facts of reality – continuously updated and completely unfiltered. He said, *I had no need for cheering dreams... facts are better than dreams.*

Transformational leaders ask questions to

> gain understanding
> find explanations
> discover a way forward.

They do not present their belief, they do not seek affirmation, they do not convey an impression that they know everything, they do not apportion blame. Rather, they invite insight, they offer opportunity for creative thinking and they instigate debate.

Collins (2001) summarised like this:

> Leadership does not mean coming up with answers and then motivating everyone to follow a messianic vision. It means having the humility to grasp the fact that you do not yet understand enough to have the answers and then to ask the questions that will lead to the best possible insights.

b) Engage in dialogue and debate, not coercion

One of the dangers of having made up one's mind in advance is that it inhibits meaningful dialogue. People invited to contribute to meaningless dialogue usually become disillusioned and give up. All consultation needs to be open and leaders need to give clear evidence that it is. One of the best ways to do so is to make plain that suggestions made have found a way into planning and policy.

Attempts to subtly influence or, worse, to try to control dialogue, will not lead to transformational change.

Dialogue may be limited because those selected to take part are chosen for their

It is the leaders' job to look at squiggly things and ask questions with others!

compliance. Some of the most productive meetings I have been in have been with colleagues with different temperaments and approaches who were able to argue loud and long, persuasively and argumentatively, openly and vigorously. Some were convergent thinkers, some very focused but willing to listen as well as speak, accepting that the intention was to address the brutal facts and find a way to transformation.

Earl and Katz support this concept;

> New ideas do not happen by osmosis. They come from facing ideas that challenge the familiar way of viewing issues.

Open dialogue and debate among everyone concerned will lead to new ideas.

c) Conduct autopsies without blame

What has gone wrong? How do you think this has happened? Where did we make the mistake? It takes a courageous person to acknowledge that something has gone wrong but if it can be done without apportioning blame then there is a chance of progress.

So, for example, the brutal fact of poor attendance figures is raised with heads of year. Data for each year group is tabled and staff invited to comment on why the situation has got worse in some year teams. Most people are quite willing to do that until the point where they sense it might be something to do with them: that is where the matter of 'without blame' arises. People will not admit any liability if they know that blame then or subsequently will be attached to them. There has to be trust which has to be constantly demonstrated. This culture can be created throughout a school but will require an insistence on challenging those who break the code by apportioning blame. It is difficult to achieve but it is an invaluable prize.

d) Build in checking mechanisms where people feel they can have their say

Most of us remember how difficult it was to speak up in class, and how intimidating we found our peers. People of all ages fear lest their contribution makes them look foolish; some people keep quiet in case their contribution makes them unpopular. Transformational leaders are so keen on finding great ideas for change and progress that they make it easy for people to risk expressing their opinion.

There are various ways this can be done in meetings where brutal facts are being confronted;

- Give people a chance to prepare in advance; not all leaders can think quickly on their feet. Some slower thinkers have ideas every bit as significant

- Allow people to submit ideas, proposals or suggestions in writing prior to the meeting

- Ask people to submit an anonymous return afterwards on how they felt about the opportunity to contribute. Take notice of what they say

- Commend, and make explicit, the value of a contribution made by a quiet participant to encourage the others

- Do not conduct the discussion in a large group. Break into smaller groups and have someone report back on each

- Ask each person to contribute 'one good idea' anonymously to address the difficult issues. Share the good ideas without attributing sources, initially at least

- Take a risk and have a 'red flag' system.

What is a red flag system? It is a method tried by Jim Collins in his classes at Stanford Business School. Collins issued MBA students with a red flag, giving them these instructions

> This is your red flag for the quarter. If you raise the red flag, the classroom will stop for you. There are no restrictions on when or how to use your red flag. You can use it to voice an observation, share an experience, present an analysis or disagree with the professor...

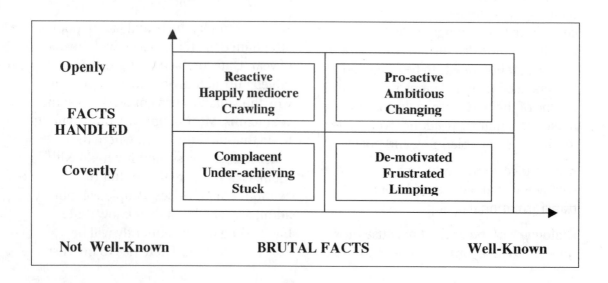

Openly	Reactive Happily mediocre Crawling	Pro-active Ambitious Changing
FACTS HANDLED		
Covertly	Complacent Under-achieving Stuck	De-motivated Frustrated Limping

| Not Well-Known | BRUTAL FACTS | Well-Known |

Some students used their flag to challenge what the professor was teaching; some brave souls even challenged the way the lesson was being delivered. It illustrates a serious intention in the mind of a transformational leader. People must be given the chance to share what they feel and the leader must check that this is happening and not just assume it is. It helps sometimes to think how that might apply for others in different positions to our own. Would a class be better if the teacher could find out what each member really thought, and acted on it? The secret lies in imaginatively making a way for it to happen.

Confronting the brutal facts is neither comfortable nor easy. Many people do not do it.

The confrontation of brutal facts may not be easy but it is essential; the ethos in the school will be affected by how thoroughly issues are faced. Change will not happen – the place is stuck and will remain so – or it is limping along because, though the brutal facts are known, they are handled secretly and staff are unaware of the real issues. For those prepared to confront the few problems they recognise, progress will be at snail's pace. But leaders who have a sense of urgency and are openly prepared to face the facts, are in a position to embark on transformational change.

However, further stages are needed to complete the process, as illustrated opposite.

SCHOOL SNAPSHOT

THE SCHOOL Firth Park Community Arts College, Sheffield
Headteacher: Mo Laycock
11-16 school, 1365 on roll, 43% on Free School Meals

25% black and ethnic minority students, many of them asylum seekers

Sixth most deprived ward in England

THE STARTING POINT 1995
76% attendance rate, falling roll, stated by Ofsted to be a school with serious weaknesses, poor, decrepit buildings

Low expectations, student, parent and staff aspirations very low

Poor community reputation

'We knew we had to change and be more successful or we would be closed down'

THE TRANSFORMATION SOUGHT
'To be the best inner city school in Sheffield'

'To get students out of their parochial and accepting rut in relation to lifestyles and low expectations'

THE ACTION TAKEN WAS:
Inspirational and realistic: it was clearly a matter of saving the school. Prioritised and single-minded

Marked by determination, and checking things out

Widely publicised 'Firth Park is Fantastic' posters everywhere

Backed by numerous letters, cards etc to all partners, regularly

Spread widely and systematically

Flexible and adjustable, in part at least

Begun initially with Mo Laycock, with nervous support from some colleagues; later it was shared by more staff at all levels

Derived from a 'passion to make a difference to the lives of our young people'

OUTCOMES
School is now full, with a waiting list

87% attendance in 2002

Arts Status in 2002

Excellent Ofsted report: Leadership described as 'inspirational and highly effective'

'The clarity with which the leaders identified the college's priorities and their commitment to continued improvement were outstanding' (Ofsted 2002)

WAS IT WORTH IT?
'When my kids performed at the National Technology Trust Conference in 2002, I was close to tears. This experience, and others, remind me we are doing the right things'

QUOTES
'Anyone can make a difference in 2-3 years. It is embedding this vision, having patience and purpose which makes the difference'

'I am passionate about my school and in gathering support for our work. I've upset some people. But this is sometimes necessary and inevitable'

SCHOOL SNAPSHOT

THE SCHOOL St Peter's R.C School, Middlesbrough
Headteacher: John Cornally
Roman Catholic Comprehensive School with 470 on roll and 48% on Free School Meals

THE STARTING POINT

There was a falling roll in 1997, with over 100 Catholic students leaving the area to attend another school some distance away. Declining reputation in and around the community. Perceived academic underperformance with 18% obtaining 5 A• to C grades at GCSE

THE TRANSFORMATION SOUGHT

A new perception of the school in the community

THE VISION

Improvement in GCSE results with particular emphasis on closing the gender gap

Developing a culture of reward and high expectations

Training and developing staff to meet the demands and challenges of sustained school improvement

Providing high quality resources for staff and pupils – specifically in ICT

THE ACTION TAKEN WAS:

Some new staff needed, a necessary precursor to change

Leadership team was too big at 8; it needed reducing to streamline decision-making

There was need to capture hearts and minds and to develop a culture of sharing

Needed to set our results against those achieved by similar children elsewhere

Needed to give staff the resources to enable them to deal with the brutal facts

The resistance to the notion of change was overcome by some of the actions above, and the appointment of new staff

OUTCOMES

Enhanced reputation of school in the community greatly reduced the migration of students

PANDA scores places school in A and B categories for KS 3 and KS 4, a major improvement

Response from community to transformation positive, supportive and encouraging

Gender gap closed at GCSE level

Highly successful Ofsted report in 2002

Development of leadership at different levels within the school

All staff now have a laptop computer

Development of shared good practice in aspects of leadership and raising standards through work with Beacon partners

Two School Achievement awards

QUOTES

'Our aim throughout was simple – improve the life chances of pupils at our school, a large number of whom come from socially disadvantaged families. This made us ready and willing to face the brutal facts as they were in order to bring about the change we sought. Our pupils are leaving with better examination results, accessing higher level post 16 courses with an increased sense of confidence and self worth. We have become a very supportive school community.'

SCHOOL SNAPSHOT

THE SCHOOL Whale Hill Primary School, Middlesbrough Headteacher: Norma Newell
Roll 508 including 78 part-time nursery children

Free School Meals 39%, 23 teachers, 15 classroom assistants

THE STARTING POINT
Staff working very hard

Ofsted (2002) praised high quality of teaching and judged relationships excellent

But 'raising standards in core subjects' still an issue

PANDA (2002) scores were poor when compared to similar schools

THE TRANSFORMATION SOUGHT
To improve performance where data said achievement was below what could be expected

THE ACTION TAKEN WAS:
To be sensitive with the presentation of the brutal facts – they felt brutal

To raise the brutal facts in connection with our moral purpose

To publicly and confidently explore together what our moral purpose was and how it related to these brutal facts

To identify for ourselves, by questions and exploration, what step changes (Rowling 2002) needed to be made to address these facts

OUTCOMES
Our corporate values strengthened

We became 'more concerned about bettering the lives of our children'

We 'wore our beliefs and values on our chests for all the world to see'

We 'began to know what we each stood for'

Standards show every evidence of significant change

WAS IT WORTH IT?
Staff 'took pride in going the extra mile' and 'giving the discretionary effort' because they say 'our children need and deserve the best'

QUOTES
The need to change, to adopt new and different approaches to teaching and learning in order to raise standards, was never viewed in terms of league table positions or the desire to out-perform others. Improvement became a natural extension of moral purpose. Understanding moral purpose made addressing the brutal facts very much easier

Chapter 5

Form the Team

The ability to work with people is as purchasable as coffee or sugar, but I'll pay more for it than any ability under the sun.
John D Rockerfeller

Transformational change does not come from a slogan or speech. It does not follow automatically if you sense a need and face some brutal facts. It begins there; but it is people who make the changes. Jack Welch worked this way,

> Change happens because you put the right people in place to make it happen. People first. Strategy and everything else next.

Making any sort of appointment these days is not easy; gone are the times when there were 30 applicants for a Head of Faculty post. It is tempting to grab the only applicant regardless of their aptitude or suitability but it is unwise. It is difficult to see how this dearth of appropriate candidates will be addressed because its root cause is reduction in the numbers entering the profession, particularly at secondary level. While it may be true that there are higher numbers entering teaching, it is also true that record numbers are leaving for a career elsewhere or para-educational initiatives like Connexions, Excellence in Cities or other supportive work. This may be worthy enough but it is taking quality people out of front-line service. Forming high quality teams when the number of high quality possibilities is so low can be extremely difficult. What can be done about it?

- Identify potential early
- Show leadership in a positive light
- Esteem core values at least as highly as skills and knowledge

- Nurture and develop leadership in a wide range of staff
- Give staff leadership responsibility early in their career
- Persuade governors to use strategies to retain the best people wherever possible
- Do not reward only for seniority
- Stretch leaders by requiring reading and research, preferably with feedbacks as training for others
- Do not recruit the wrong people for the bus: it is easier to get them on than off

When it is possible to progress up the pay scales without adding significant responsibility, why would anyone want to become a leader? That is becoming an increasingly common argument: it is understandable. Yet leadership is a brilliant calling, influential, rewarding and fulfilling. Leaders themselves need to model it well so that others are inspired to face the challenge themselves. Undoubtedly, there are perceptions of leadership putting people off facing that challenge. In research undertaken in Canada, where the same recruitment problems have emerged too, the six highest ranked 'dissatisfiers' damping teachers' enthusiasm for leadership roles were:

- The inadequate time given to plan mandated change

- Too many curriculum changes initiated

- Too little time available to work with students

- Not enough in-school support

- Too much time required to do the job properly

- Too few resources to complete the task successfully

The researchers found these disincentives at all levels of leadership throughout an organisation. It is futile to

When it is possible to progress up the pay scales without adding significant responsibility, why would anyone want to become a leader?

bemoan the lack of emerging leadership if the existing leaders do not take great care to minimise these disincentives within their own organisation: we need to make our actions match our rhetoric.

The penultimate layer in levels of leadership categorised by the Stanford team was a level four leader; called by Collins the 'Genius with a thousand helpers': the highest order transformational leaders, level five, built a superior team capable of introducing and sustaining transformational change. Evidence from research shows that great charismatic leaders are difficult to follow and leave a situation drifting back often towards mediocrity. The team concept is clearly crucial.

John Kotter explains this further:

> Producing major change in an organisation is not just about signing up one charismatic leader. You need a group – a team – to be able to drive the change. One person, even a terrific charismatic leader, is never strong enough to make all this happen.

> Individuals alone, no matter how competent or charismatic, never have all the assets needed to overcome tradition and inertia, except in very small organisations.

People are indeed the most important asset. Wrong! The right people are the most important asset.

David Nassef, of Pitney Bowes, has clear selection procedures to ensure his company get the right people on the bus,

We don't just look at experience. We want to know: who are they? Why are they? We find out who they are by asking them why they made decisions in their life. The answers to these questions give us insight into their core values.

At this time when applicants for senior posts in education are at a low ebb, choice is often limited. This is sad, when the leaders in our institutions need to be very able and have transformational potential. Some leaders however have inherited well-established teams; they have no choice. This difficult problem will be discussed later.

How do you select a team?
The qualities needed in a team depend on the skills and abilities of the present team membership, but there are some essential qualities that would guarantee the right people were on the bus.

a) People with beliefs and values
David Nassef said that what was needed was people with 'core values'; Fullan called it Moral Purpose. The team may be diverse in a multitude of ways but transformational teams have a common set of values. They may be articulated in slightly different ways, but there is no doubting the inner motivation to make a difference.

Karl Albrecht (1994) reckons that there is a human need for such core values to underpin endeavour if maximum effect is to be achieved,

> In many ways the crisis today is a crisis of meaning. People are not sure of themselves because they no longer understand the why behind the what. They no longer have the sense that things are well-defined and that hard work will lead to success. More and more people have feelings of doubt and uncertainty about the future of their organisations, and consequently about their careers and future. Those

who would aspire to leadership...must not underestimate the depth of the human need for meaning. It is the most fundamental human craving, an appetite that will not go away.

In this respect, things have not changed since 1994: perhaps the season of direction – being told what to do without a clear understanding of why – has contributed to this 'crisis' of meaning. It is important that hearts and minds are together in those who are seeking to make transformational change. Recognition that this is as much a fundamental craving in those who work alongside leaders as in the leaders themselves would be a great advantage.

b) Passion
Fullan uses words with emotional strength like *passionately* and *intensely* to convey depth of feeling and commitment. Jack Welch concurs.

> Whenever I asked one of my leadership classes what constitutes an A player, it always made me happiest to see the first hand go up and say, 'Passion'. For me, intensity covers a lot of sins. If there is one characteristic all winners share, it's that they care more than anyone else. No detail is too small to sweat or too large to dream. It's something that comes from deep inside.

c) Aspiration
It is really helpful to have a team with members who have ambition, longing, yearning to succeed and aspiration to be significant for others. I was no academic, but I remember distinctly that as a young man taking finals at university, I set myself the ambition of achieving a class of degree that would make the professor say, 'You did better than I thought you could'. It does not matter how highly we achieve, so long as we aspire to stretch ourselves beyond our limits. Teams with such aspirant

members are lively, alert, proactive, energised and, almost always, transformational.

d) Team people

The qualities in b) and c) are personal qualities. Just as important are qualities that make people team people; the leader enjoys having such staff around and feels encouraged by them. Warren Bennis was right when he said

> The leader finds greatness in the group, and she helps the members to find greatness in themselves.

For most people there is immense satisfaction in being part of a team. If it is possible to select people who fit well then it is wise to do it; if not, there will need to be specific training to develop the team ethos because so much potential for change will be lost without it.

e) Determination

Transformational change does not happen overnight: battles will be lost on the way. Admiral Jim Stockdale was the highest-ranking officer in the 'Hanoi Hilton' prisoner-of-war camp in Vietnam. His exploits became legendary; his reminiscences on his experiences were extraordinarily powerful. There were men with a wide variety of temperaments incarcerated in Vietnam. Stockdale explained that many of the men who survived were the men with faith that they would get out. However, he pointed out that they were not the optimists – 'We'll be out by Christmas'- then, when they weren't – 'We'll be out by Easter' – and when they weren't – 'We'll be out by fall'. Stanford said that many men like that never did come out. They perished with shattered dreams; they died of a broken heart. The ones who did come out of Vietnam were often men who said, 'No matter how long it takes, we are going to see it through'.

> *Realistic leaders are objective enough to minimise illusions. They understand that self-deception can cost them their vision*
>
> *Bill Easum*

Stockdale put it starkly

> You must never confuse faith that you will prevail in the end – which you can never afford to lose – with the discipline to confront the most brutal facts of your current reality, whatever they may be.

Such determination is required in transformational leaders, courage to face brutal facts and determination that change will be seen through to a conclusion.

Unless a positive reality permeates team life, the transformational vision will be seriously impaired.

f) Challenge

Always use your best people on exploiting opportunities, not on dealing with problems: that was Jack Welch's philosophy. It runs counter to life in many schools where managing the crisis absorbs endless hours of the time of our best leaders. Problems do have to be solved, but creating opportunities is energising and inspiring and must not be sacrificed. According to Rob Parsons, *'the best leaders do not want a bigger office, they want a bigger challenge.'* That attitude offers all sorts of potential for change.

Jim Collins and other celebrated leaders in business and industry have been teaching that it is *'always who, not what'.* Some of the qualities that transformational people should and

Qualities creating potential	Qualities creating problems
Ability Commitment Enthusiasm Conviction Determination Aspiration Clarity Persuasiveness Teamwork Diversity	Superficiality Insecurity Double-mindedness Half-heartedness Cynicism World-weariness Gloom Defeatism Acquiescence

should not have are shown in the figure above.

It is helpful if transformational leaders include people with creative, imaginative inclination who are constantly thinking of new ideas. Often such ideas come to nothing, or emerge redefined, but they are a brilliant catalyst to start the thinking. In teamwork, the image of the last five years has been the flight of geese. Let me introduce you to the bee:

> A worker bee finds a major source of pollen, flies back to the hive, and performs a dance that shows the other bees the direction of the pollen source. At least 85% of them do. The other 15% do not follow the swarm. They look for other sources of pollen, and when they find it , the story starts all over again.

Teams need the 15%; these people will not always be on the leadership team but they need to be encouraged and developed; their skills are valuable. It is gratifying if you can find 85% of staff prepared to follow a new idea, but it is necessary to have some key staff capable of finding *more* new ideas if transitional change is to be advanced; it is equally important to dedicate quality time to allow them to do it. Occasionally bright new ideas are stumbled on in the course of a busy routine; more often they emerge as creative thinkers spend time dedicated to researching new possibilities.

What can be done if I have inherited a team already?

Business and industry appears far more ruthless than educationalists could be, or would want to be, when they discover they have the wrong people on the bus. However, it remains a significant problem if the team in place is ill equipped to deal with the emerging realities from sensing a need and facing brutal facts. Something has to be done.

It is essential to avoid the 'It's them, not me' complex. This is a situation where it is most easily felt; yet, most transformational leaders attempt to make change to their senior leadership teams with the genuine belief that it is possible; indeed the transformation of a leadership team is as good a place to start as any.

The process begins by sensing the need for significant change; a recognition that things are not as they should be and that if matters are left unattended transformation simply will not happen. Often the team is as aware of that as is the leader of the team: members feel ill at ease, uncomfortable, unfulfilled, frustrated, inadequate, trapped or anxious; debilitating emotions all. The headteacher feels frustrated and limited by the capability of the team she has inherited. As a consequence, transformation is slowed, if not halted, and matters will only get worse. Something should be done but often it is not.

Tackling situations like this require the brutal facts to be assembled; the problems need to be exposed, and the processes defined earlier needs to be introduced.

Questions need to be asked.

- Do you think that, as we are, transformational change can be made?

- Why do you think we are not moving forward on issue X?

- In what ways are we responsible for the changes not happening?

- How might we change our roles to make change more achievable?

The leader may believe she knows what has to be done, her experience makes that clear, but the process of *questions not answers* followed by *autopsies without blame* is an essential pre-requisite to any action. Members need to be free to say what they feel.

Beyond this team engagement, personal conversations inevitably follow with individual members; in most schools the team do not make the big decisions, the leader does. These decisions are influenced by the outcomes of the debate and dialogue and the autopsies without blame; but they can be extremely sensitive matters. The team must be aware that a situation where transformation is being hindered has to change. There are four ways to do this.

Re-energising

Finding new energy is sometimes called a 'new lease of life' or 'second wind'. I remember it well from days running

across country. One minute it seemed that all energy had gone; the next that fresh supplies had arrived and there was hope again. This often happens to de-motivated colleagues when there is a change of leadership in a school; clearly, then, it is not all the fault of the people who feel de-energised. Re-energising can happen simply as a result of renewed interest in a person's personal progress, or because of the offer of a new opportunity. People do respond if they have faith placed in them, rising to unexpected heights. Such possibilities for transforming colleagues need to be discovered while the existing leaders still remain: causes of blockages need tracing, wherever that is possible.

Retraining

Problems emerging from debate and dialogue indicate that the issues are not too serious. Systematic, planned personal development may breathe new life and vitality into weary team members. It is essential, in such cases, that there are agreed outcomes expected as a consequence of measures of this kind, so that evident change is brought about by the process. A clear action plan, with specific targets focused on areas where change is required, needs to be agreed with accountability introduced into it. Support and encouragement will offer a higher probability of success. It may work.

Redefining

Getting the right people on the bus may be achieved simply by moving their seat; this is the least painful option. Someone may have been leader of the pastoral team and impeded the necessary changes, or a Key Stage co-ordinator so poor on motivation and inspiration that their role is counter-productive. Where it is possible to agree what their strengths are and redefine their role to maximise them, these strengths would be a blessing to everybody. It is always desirable to ensure that there is no loss of self-esteem in this process. This may mean some concession being made by the leader, for example, by giving them a new position of responsibility along with their redefined role.

Tricia was Head of Science and also responsible for Careers Education: in her subject she had run out of both ideas and energy, and, though this was not very apparent, it caused her great concern and anxiety. The Science team had long since given up on any meaningful insights from Tricia in their meetings and found her contributions unhelpful, even obstructive. Ways were found to increase the Careers Education role, with the challenge to extend and expand the service while at the same time handing over the academic leadership to a new team member. It is not always possible to devise solutions that leave everyone happy.

Removing
Business and industry are used to this way of operating. In his leadership teams, Jack Welch had leaders categorised A, B or C, generally in the ration 20%, 70% and 10%, pleasant for those in the A grades but uncomfortable if you happened to be C.

> I learned a lot in my early days about moving people out. It's the toughest and most difficult thing we ever do. It is never easy and it does not become easier.

> If I have learned anything at all about making it easier, it is seeing to it that no one should ever be surprised when they are asked to leave. By the time I met with managers I was about to replace, I would have had at least two or three conversations to express my disappointment and to give them a chance to turn things round.

Welch argues that initially there is disappointment and shock, but that

Redefine roles of those who should *do the job.* *Create space for the appointment of those who* will *do the job.*

more often than not, there is relief. He reckons that he has *seen many people go on to better and happier lives after leaving jobs that just weren't working. All of us have responsibility to try to make that happen.*

That is a different world to the educational environment where custom and practice has been altogether opposed to such severe tactics. Welch concedes that *I've been lucky enough all my life to work for a company with resources enough to soften the blow.* Leaders in education have never been convinced that money can soften blows like that, even if they had it.

However our world may be changing. As well as Charles Clarke's proposal about poor heads of 'taking them out', there is the interesting suggestion in the Leadership Incentive Grant guidance that money may be used to remove blockages in the middle management structure. It does sound a lot closer to Welch than what we have heard before.

Despite the in-built resistance to draconian measures, it has to be conceded that something has to be done if and when other strategies have failed. Competence procedures make it possible to make change but they are so slow and cumbersome, so designed to support the staff that most leaders give up before they begin. The amount of transformation that is being stalled by situations like this must be enormous.

The conclusion seems to be that removal is so difficult as to be almost impossible: subtler, more sophisticated approaches seem the only alternatives for most leaders who find themselves in this position. Sadly, while the complicated political debate goes on, young people who would benefit from proactive transformational change are being affected.

Forming the team is important though it is clearly essential that the team should be effective. Hackman (2002) emphasised five conditions in which teams will be effective:

- It is a *real* team and not just a team in name only.

A real team is where each member cares about, inter-relates with and supports the others. It is a team in which discussion, debate and dialogue are meaningful, where respect reigns and collaboration is paramount. Rivalry is resisted, or, if it exists, is positive and friendly. Every member feels a sense of significance with a real team. A leader's role is to ensure that these things are happening, since they will be challenged from time to time.

- There is a compelling sense of direction for its work

An effective team knows where it is going and what it is doing, as well as feeling a deep inner corporate commitment to an agreed agenda, motivated as often as not by a shared moral purpose. It is not just about clearly defined job descriptions, important as they are; it is more about each member playing their own part, keeping their shape, standing together though doing different things and working towards desirable goals.

- The team has an enabling structure facilitating rather than impeding teamwork

The team that is formed is a living force but the skeleton on which it is based is important: the structure of its organisation is that skeleton. Some teams are all skeleton with no life, no muscle, no energy. Meetings are held but are routine and sterile. By contrast meetings can be full of lively ideas and creativity but without regularity, follow-through or enough routine to make things happen. No one wants to see a skeleton but without one there will not be much worthwhile action.

- A supportive organisational context exists in which the team thrives

An air of mystery surrounds the work of some senior leadership teams. Sometimes, it is deliberately created by the leadership, though more often it is as a result of inattention to communication. Teams functioning in an open way and having highly developed communication and interaction certainly thrive. A supportive organisational context can be developed.

- Expert coaching in teamwork pays enormous dividends

Forming the team is crucial but servicing it, keeping it highly tuned and ensuring its smooth operation, is equally vital. Leaving people with a degree of autonomy and independence within a team is necessary and productive. A leader's function is to watch over the team and the way it is interacting so that interventions, encouragement and personal support can be offered to guarantee effectiveness. The team may not all be star players but skilled coaches are capable of building brilliant teams.

Nicolo Machiavelli, the Florentine diplomat, took an interesting perspective on this

> The first method of estimating the intelligence of a ruler (leader) is to look at the men (and women) he has around him.

Wise transformational leaders devise what plans they can to form the right team to do the job, then they show the way.

SCHOOL SNAPSHOT

THE SCHOOL Lent Rise School, Buckinghamshire
Headteacher: Brenda Bigland
Ages 4 to 11, Infant and Junior School, Free School Meals 11%

THE STARTING POINT
New headteacher 1991, school with falling roll and deficit budget

Pupil numbers being recruited to the school dangerously low

The team of teachers and leaders had worked together for a long time and had run out of belief that change was possible

THE TRANSFORMATION SOUGHT
Restoration of confidence in staff, renewal of reputation of the school to stop the falling roll and create a centre of excellence

THE TEAM APPROACH
First the headteacher needed to demonstrate personal commitment to the challenge of leading the school and to exemplify the standards that were being expected, without rocking the boat of existing staff too much

Attempts were made to 'lift the environment' and create a spirit of hope amongst partners

There was resistance from some at first; the new head is a 'pain in the butt'

The headteacher used her own appraisal to ask questions of parents and others about what they wanted in their school; she then showed the results of the survey openly to encourage staff to see that partners believed they could achieve so much more. The questions that she had used had been agreed in advance by staff and so had authenticity

Some staff responded to seeing what parents wanted and began to offer to take on activities that had been suggested: peer pressure developed that trend

The headteacher raised the issues of low standards and was approached by a young member of staff about whether she could help to do something about it

The head invited her round for a meal and talked over what might be done: she ultimately became the team leader and four years later became Assistant Headteacher

Another meal with a few more staff lead to the development of a policy on assessment

It took two years to get the right people in place to create the teams to make the changes

Some staff moved on, offering the opportunity to find the best blend of talent in the teams: it was a key principle to set partnership on the agenda from the beginning with these new staff at their appointment

OUTCOMES
From Ofsted report 2002, 90% teaching very good or excellent, leadership across the school excellent, no issues reported

Leadership is expected and demonstrated at every level across the school

Roll has increased and the reputation of the school in the community is outstanding

WAS IT WORTH IT?
Yes. The school has changed beyond all recognition and now has a national reputation for good practice

QUOTES
'I expect staff to be able to tell me where they are going and how they plan to get there. I expect all staff to be prepared to be leaders in their own way'

SCHOOL SNAPSHOT

THE SCHOOL Seaton Burn Community College, North Tyneside Principal: Stephen Prandle
Ages 11 to 18, Comprehensive School, Free School Meals 19%, 55 teachers

THE STARTING POINT
Recruitment and retention in sixth form needed safeguarding and increasing

Local attractive alternatives made it necessary to offer something different and attractive

The college needed a unique selling point to attract and expand

THE TRANSFORMATION SOUGHT
To develop a specialism in Business and Enterprise

To transform the culture to create a pervasive Business and Enterprise ethos

THE TEAM APPROACH:
Decided to create a new team entirely dedicated to preparing the bid and influencing the culture

Selected two from four members of Senior Leadership Team (SLT) according to aptitude

The two not selected agreed to widen their remit to take in roles vacated by those who were selected

Care taken to retain support of whole SLT

A new Head of Faculty had enthusiasm for this development and was invited to bring her highly relevant skills to the team. One other member was needed with background in Mathematics. The incumbent Head of Faculty was marginally involved (and soon moved on to an Advanced Skills Teacher post). This led to an advertisement, then a re-advertisement on a higher salary, until a person was found with expertise in mathematics but, also, experience of specialist school bidding. An LEA advisor joined the team and, upon retirement, became their consultant, bringing experience and wider understanding to the proceedings

Meetings were structured so that each member met with the headteacher at least once every week, for six months, rather than having whole team meetings weekly

The team was designed to include a 'Big Ideas' person, a completer-finisher especially involved in fundraising, a creative thinker querying and challenging, and a consultant: all coordinated by the principal, who had a coaching role with each member in turn

The team was involved in writing the bid, but, just as significantly, were designated the role of changing the ethos of the college

Their work included the development of an Enterprise culture, encouraging students in Enterprise activities and in changing the emphasis in existing departments to include an Enterprise focus

OUTCOMES
The bid has been presented and is assisted by the designation by the Excellence in Cities Partnership as a priority school

As many as 30 different new student Enterprise groups have emerged over the past six months, guided and supported by the team

WAS IT WORTH IT?
'Unquestionably. It has been a good process finding and using competencies of a close knit team, and through them, the competences of the whole staff and student body.'

QUOTES
'I found myself, as principal, being the centre of everything and yet the expert in nothing'

'I did not want a deputy taken out by this bidding process who would write something in isolation. I wanted consultation, discussion and involvement because I believed that was the way to change the ethos of the College'

Chapter 6

Show the way

Effective leaders take time and trouble to make their philosophies explicit for themselves and explain them to parents and students; the foundation of a leader's work and corporate life is an acceptance of shared values.

HMI Ten Good Schools 1977

It is tempting to put vision before people. This is a mistake. It is people who make transformational change – and it has to be the right people, which is why Forming the Team comes before Showing the Way.

However, there is no mistaking the importance of knowing the way and of being able to show that way clearly to others. As Henry Kissinger put it: *The task of the leader is to get her people from where they are to where they have not been.*

Some will think they know the way, some will resent being told again, some will think they have better things to do.

Soon after he had started driving at 18, his company sent my son to Warrington on his first assignment. It was exciting for him, though as seems typical with young men, he did not talk about it much. He did not even ask for directions and, believing discretion was the better part of valour, I offered none. He got there. It took longer than any of us expected but he got there. He worked the whole week and set off for Middlesbrough at 2 pm on Friday. At 6 pm I received a phone call from him. 'Dad,' said the plaintive voice, 'where's the Humber Bridge?' He thought he knew the way and had no map with him. He missed the turn onto the A1. He learned a lesson, and so did I.

Mistakes of such a kind in educational or other organisational leadership can ruin transformational change. Almost all

Know where you are
Know where you want to be
Know some landmarks on
the way
Have something written
down
Have a contact to talk to

schools have vision statements but they sound rather like 'I'm going to Middlesbrough'. It is easy to miss the way.

What is vision?

Vision was defined by Karl Albrecht (1994) as;

> a shared image of what we want the enterprise to be or become... an aiming point for a future orientation. The vision implies an element of noble purpose and big values, of something considered especially worthwhile.

Burt Nannis (1992) saw it differently – as

> a realistic, credible, attractive future for your organisation; an idea so energising that in effect it jump-starts the future by calling forth the skills, talents and resources to make it happen, and a signpost pointing the way for all who need to understand what the organisation is and where it intends to go.

Tony Blair and George Bush have coined a new phrase for the future. They appear to be calling what we called once vision for the future, the *road map*.

Vision is a picture of the future, generally with some clearly defined moral purpose. Most of us appreciate the journey more if we know why we are making it. Knowing the way, and showing the way, is important because it

- clarifies where we are going and why

- gets people fired up and ready to go

- encourages people to move together

The culture of an organisation is seriously affected by the clarity of the vision. Every group of headteachers with whom I have been engaged in training have put 'clarity and imparting of vision' as the chief responsibility that they have. Even though research shows that putting the right people in place is even more important it certainly has immense significance.

Signs on the way are a necessary part of moving vision into transformational change (see diagram below).

Where vision is strong but no one can see any change resulting from it, the vision will be aborted. One school I knew had a well-defined and articulate vision that their school should have a swimming pool, but nothing happened for months and there were no signs, no progress and no explanation – the vision was aborted.

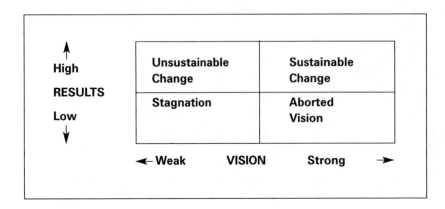

	Weak VISION	Strong
High RESULTS	Unsustainable Change	Sustainable Change
Low	Stagnation	Aborted Vision

More painfully, my own school has had a seriously transformational vision for seven years; that it should change status from 11 to 16 to 11 to 18. It has been well planned and well articulated, but it has met fierce political resistance. Nothing has happened yet. One day it may, but neither this vision, nor any other, can survive forever with few results in evidence: knowing when to abort a vision is another thing. Nelson Mandela waited a long time before signs of significant change, but thanks to the strength of his vision he managed not to abort.

Where vision is weak and results are low, nothing happens except that people become listless, frustrated and purposeless which is not a healthy scene. Occasionally achievements are high but vision is weak and in these cases the change will be unsustainable.

Where there are positive signs linked to strong vision there is the potential for major sustainable change. Should the vision weaken however sustainability will be threatened. To guarantee transformation there has to be strong vision. But vision is often a '*hopelessly vague listing of qualities*', as Kotter puts it. Typical are statements like: the school has a vision to

> maintain good progress
> create a healthy environment
> foster good employee relationships.

Such statements never provide clear direction and turn off everyone but extreme idealists.

Some vision has no underlying clear moral purpose. It is shooting in the dark. Though the words seem fine there is no transparent feeling or sense of purpose. Confucius remarked that

> Radical changes require adequate authority. A person must have inner strength as well as influential position. What she does must correspond with a higher truth.

poor vision is:

too vague

purposeless

too wordy

There will be various interpretations of what that truth should be. Though this is important, what matters most is that there is some clearly understood and agreed moral purpose underpinning vision for successful transformation. Heather Du Quesnay (2003) explained her belief:

> Teachers have almost a victim mentality: a sense of being locked into somebody else's agenda. If we cannot recapture the creative spirit that brings people into the teaching profession, it could lead to 'melt down' for public education. Leaders must give those in the profession a greater sense of purpose, derived from moral and ethical principles. The more government initiatives hurled at teachers, the more important that senior leaders of schools create that sense of greater purpose.

This is a recurrent theme amongst key academics talking about educational change. Leaders need to ensure it is happening.

A third danger is that vision is too wordy. Vision statements that occupy pages of space very often do not occupy space in people's hearts or heads. If you cannot describe your vision to someone in five minutes and get their interest, you have no vision that will be capable of effecting change.

Lady Marie Stubbs retired from successful headship in August 2001 with no intention of returning to school leadership; then, out of the blue, she was invited in 2002 to take the helm at St George's Roman Catholic Secondary

School in Maida Vale, London. This is the school where the headteacher, Philip Lawrence was stabbed to death in 1995. She took up the challenge, and recalls the day she spoke to the students to communicate the vision, 'I told them the past is over, from now on St George's is going to be a place where we all pull together, learn together and take part in enjoyable events and outings'. She concluded by telling the students there was to be a special day when we will 'have a May Ball at a top hotel': and she was as good as her word. Her vision was not too wordy and it was clear and full of hope, specific and supportive. It caught on and transformation was underway.

Any vision that is hard to visualise is not likely to attract support or commitment.

To produce transformation a vision must have some essential characteristics.

It must be able to be:

Imagined	Desired
Achieved	Specified
Adapted	Understood
Talked about	Measured

It is not hard to see how Marie Stubbs' vision matches those characteristics. The students could imagine a great deal of what she said to them, and could see the benefits.

The movie actor, Jim Carrey, used visualisation to brilliant effect. He knew that his ability to twist and contort his body into unusual positions plus his comic skills made him a unique talent. Carrey had many challenges before he hit the big time. Long before he did so, he wrote himself a cheque for ten million dollars 'For Services Rendered' and kept it hidden. When times were tough, he would sit on a hillside above Los Angeles and imagine himself a movie star. He would reread his cheque and visualise the dawn of the new day. His cheque for The Mask was for more than a million dollars; and the date when it was signed was close to the one

If there is no appeal to excitement or self-interest people will be reluctant to make the journey

on the cheque he had made out to himself. Vision has to be able to be imagined, linked to the reality of talent and resources and be sufficiently stretching to be challenging.

Vision has also to point to an outcome that people want. If there is no measure of self-interest in the destination then people are going to be reluctant to embark on it.

Rather than stretching people too far, there has to be a sense of realism, not some statement that everyone knows to be unachievable. The notion of 'aspirational targets' set for schools at all Key Stages seems to me to be problematic and they have been called 'fanciful' (by David Hart and others). People resist being invited to take journeys that are merely flights of fancy. I know headteachers who believe some of their Key Stage targets to be totally unrealistic and so ignore them.

With a grandfather who was a gamekeeper, there was no way I could escape a sortie into the world of shooting. It was singularly unsuccessful, not least because I would shoot at pheasants 100 yards away. Father would ask if I thought I had a cannon and the pheasant was rarely troubled by my efforts. I envisioned success but had no chance. I have learned a lesson for life.

Vision must also be specific and avoid vagueness. It must also be adaptable. Flexibility can be an enemy of transformational change because it gives people the opportunity to pursue a different vision. Adaptability is different. Teachers need a chance to put something of their own personality into the achievement of vision.

It is possible to strait-jacket teachers over teaching and learning. Telling staff what the vision is is one thing but telling them exactly what to do and when is quite another. The mark two version of the Literacy Strategy has more to commend it than the first because it allows for a little more freedom of interpretation. The mark one version was much more prescriptive, not least because there was a fear that flexibility would ruin the vision. Leaders need to be clear and specific over vision, but not so restrictive that people feel they can have no part in it.

If it is clear and concise, it is likely to be intelligible. Ideally, a vision so catches the imagination that it is talked about. How often is the vision of our schools the subject of day-to-day conversation? It needs to be.

So vision needs to be:

- **brief**
- **clear**
- **simple**
- **picturesque**
- **worth going for**
- **having wide appeal**
- **topical**
- **purposeful**

Marie Stubbs and her team chose the slogan for their vision as 'Moving Forward Together in 2000'. It had the virtue of being brief, clear and simple. It was posted around the school, visible, purposeful and highly relevant.

It was election year when we began looking at the performance of students in Nunthorpe School at the C/D borderline. Students capable of

If you want to hit the target, keep in range

achieving a grade C but apparently unlikely to do so were identified and strategies devised to get them there. We called these students Key Marginals, a term stolen from electioneering. Key Marginals were seats where there was a battle for victory and that would make a difference to the overall position of the political party. We published the names of these students in the staff room, with their present achievement set against our aspirations for them, under the slogan 'Get these and Get a Record'. We thought it was simple, brief, clear and topical. It caught on and was talked about. We use it still. Did it work? Of the 47 students identified as not having much chance of 5 A* to C, 42 achieved it! We were happy and so were they.

Charles Clarke (2003) has talked about 'leadership being at all levels of the organisation rather than in heroic leadership models, which can be counterproductive'. Collins' argument was that the 'genius with a thousand helpers' will get things done but the better way is to have leaders who embrace and release others. Max DePree (1992) said much the same '*Your vision must be large enough to contain multitudes*'. For all that, the driving force behind a vision is often one person, some significant catalyst in showing the way.

Warren Bennis (1994) observed that *Just as no great painting has ever been created by a committee, no great vision has*

POSSIBLE future:	Things which could happen, although many are unlikely
PROBABLE future:	Things which will happen, unless something is done to turn things around
PREFERRED future:	Things that you prefer to have happen and/or what you would like to plan to happen

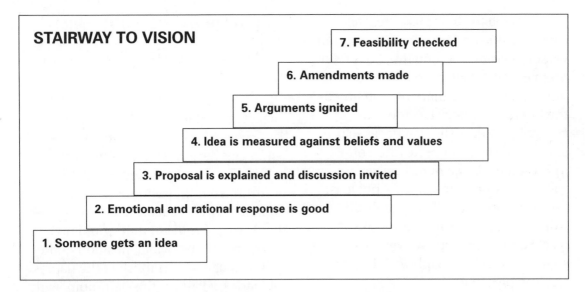

STAIRWAY TO VISION

7. Feasibility checked

6. Amendments made

5. Arguments ignited

4. Idea is measured against beliefs and values

3. Proposal is explained and discussion invited

2. Emotional and rational response is good

1. Someone gets an idea

emerged from the herd. The development of the vision needs wide ownership but often the driving initiating force lies in one person. Beare (2001) suggested that teams consider the possible future, the probable future and the preferred future.

Once the team is formed, how is the vision created? Time must be set aside to formulate the visions guiding the transformational change.

■ Having an idea

Anyone can have an idea for the transformational vision and it is important that staff feel able to communicate ideas they have. The fact that the idea for the vision has come from someone not in the leadership team is a great strength. Harry Truman said that *You can accomplish anything in life, so long as you don't mind who gets the credit.* A good idea from a member of staff may be the spark that lights the fire. It does not matter who is credited with it.

Leaders recognise the potential of an idea, note it, think about it and share it. Ideas appear from nowhere: some of the best ideas I have discovered came in the middle of the night (that is why I keep a notepad by the bed), in casual conversation with others, from reading books or attending conferences. Rarely can ideas be lifted from others without adaptation after reflection. Ideas are

powerful mechanisms for transformational change.

Fullan (2003) talks of DOVE thinking when ideas are being put forward:

Defer judgement: accept all ideas, list everything, evaluate later

Opt for original and offbeat: anything goes, especially different and crazy ideas

Vast numbers of ideas are best: get many ideas, the more the better

Expand by association: piggyback off each other's ideas

■ Emotional Engagement

Motivation is an emotional word. The greatest ideas generate excitement and feeling which is to be encouraged. There then begins what Jack Welch calls 'wallowing'. I've done plenty, but never called it by that name. He defines wallowing as:

> Getting a group of people round a table, regardless of their rank, to wrestle with a particularly tough issue. Stewing on it from every angle, flushing out everyone's thinking, but not drawing an immediate conclusion.

This strategy is particularly appropriate in handling vision. Vital in the process are constant checks on what the fundamental beliefs and values are. These should not be omitted.

In some collaborative work I have been involved in, the brutal facts were straightforward: standards of achievement were too low. The discussion, following the consideration of these facts, introduced the idea that the parents of students in some schools in more privileged areas were prepared to pay for private coaching, especially in the core subjects. One-to-one coaching appeared beneficial to the children's performances. Someone had the bright idea that their own school, in an area of social disadvantage, ought to be able to do the same. Then the wallowing began. There was excitement about the possibility of a new transformational initiative which could make a huge difference. Someone proposed holding one-to-three private coaching sessions for the young people of that school but commented that because parents in the more advantaged areas paid that gave their scheme strength. The belief was that the parents paying helped therefore parents should pay but this conflicted with the values of those discussing the issue, who believed that parents should not. Impasse! But not for that group who squared the circle. They set upon a scheme in which parents would pay a bond and if their child attended all the private coaching sessions, they would get the money back. They paid and yet they did not pay. That is the creative power of a wallowing group which is underpinned by the fundamental importance of moral purpose and of beliefs and values.

■ Discussion and Dialogue bring ideas to maturity

A team that shares in that way will know the way, and will be in a position to show the way. Once the vision is known and established, it is essential to understand the process of moving it forward. The same process applies in deciding where to go for a family holiday. Someone has an idea which generates emotional engagement, discussion and dialogue. Inevitably it is checked out for feasibility, whether it matches the requirements of all the family and whether it can be afforded. The road map, the vision, is completed. We know the route. Now how are we intending to get there?

SCHOOL SNAPSHOT

THE SCHOOL Archbishop Holgate's School, York

Headteacher: John Harris

11-16 school, 750 on roll, 13% on Free School Meals, 48 teachers

THE STARTING POINT

Headteacher arrived in 1992 when the school had a falling roll and had achieved 19% of students obtaining 5 A to C in 1991. Morale amongst staff was low, response from the community weak.

The school was Voluntary Controlled

THE TRANSFORMATION SOUGHT

To give the school a new distinctively community based approach with an increase in the links with the church connection in order to change the ethos. The possibility of becoming Voluntary Aided (VA) seemed to offer the opportunity for this transformation

ESTABLISHING THE VISION:

The possibility offered by VA was investigated by the headteacher. The idea of change was 'drip fed' to the Leadership Team and discussions and arguments about pros and cons ensued for several months. Patience was required. The headteacher made clear that a concensus of the Leadership Team would be required, without it, the proposal would not be considered further

The issue of the beliefs and values of all the Leadership Team were paramount

Draft after draft was prepared, discussed and amended until agreement was unanimous to establish change to VA as the vision. Once the SLT had agreed, a set of strategic aims were written, discussed, amended and then agreed by the SLT

The same process was repeated with staff, first by drip feed, raising possibilities, listening to responses

The aim was to align key staff 'bit by bit'. Staff were found who had experience of working in VA schools and their opinion sought out by SLT. These staff were invited to discuss their views with other staff. Attempts were made at intervals to judge staff response to the possibilities being explored

Complications caused for staff contracts were raised openly and discussed. Research was done and contracts used in other schools used to demonstrate the issues and to allay fears

Unions were invited to discuss all concerns and to make suggestions

Great sensitivity was needed

OUTCOMES

Voluntary Aided Status was confirmed over four years after the initial opportunity was first introduced. The morale of staff was affected markedly so that there began to be an eagerness to be involved in the new opportunity. Since then, the roll has increased significantly and in 2002 57% of students achieved 5 or more 'A• to C grades

WAS IT WORTH IT?

The change in staff and parental perceptions alone make it worthwhile. 'I hear Archbishop's is on the move' and 'It's lovely to work in an atmosphere like that' are just two of the statements made by staff since VA instigated a significant transformation at the school

QUOTES

You need to be sensitive in situations like this to a variety of stakeholders views. You also need to keep the Vision clear

SCHOOL SNAPSHOT

THE SCHOOL Houghton Kepier School, Houghton-le-Spring Headteacher: Sue Hyland
11-16 comprehensive school, 1360 on roll, 31% on Free School Meals

GCSE achievement 35% obtain 5 or more C or better

THE STARTING POINT
New headteacher in January 1999. Ofsted report in second week of January placed school in serious weaknesses. One of several issues was that leadership and management were weak, lacking clear perspective and focus, properly designated responsibility or time to manage

THE TRANSFORMATION SOUGHT
To address this issue in particular in order to create a leadership team that was smaller and more effective with appropriately designated responsibilities and accountability structures in place

ESTABLISHING THE VISION
The headteacher conducted individual meetings with all senior staff members to hear their views on how things were

A social event was held at the headteacher's house to attempt to build relationships before addressing the difficult issues

A two-day residential conference was held for senior team members still in post when roles and responsibilities were discussed in general, before agreement was reached on the specific brief that the members of the new senior team would have

At this residential one of the starting points was the report provided by Ofsted on the present state of leadership and management

Despite there being fewer posts than people available to fill them, concensus was reached on what was best for the school

This became the vision, the end point of the route map

There followed application and appointment procedures to fill posts agreed

OUTCOMES
Ofsted returned in 2001 and reported a 'strong leadership team'

Regional Centres for NPQH use the school as a model of good leadership practice

There is now truly delegated responsibility to the leadership team and trust in the team

The headteacher was awarded 'Headteacher of the Year 2001'

WAS IT WORTH IT?
The whole process was gratifying, staff sense the team's togetherness and draw strength from it

QUOTES
It is not possible to transform a school the size of this one without team coherence and commitment. To reach a place where the team are happy, constructive with no point scoring each supporting the other is most stimulating and encouraging. It is also immensely helpful to the school, indeed crucial to success

Chapter 7

Spread the Word

Precision of communication is important, more important than ever, in our era of hair-trigger balances, when a false or misunderstood word may create as much disaster as a sudden thoughtless act.
James Thurber

Once the leadership team has worked together to find the way and show it, it becomes imperative that the transformational vision is transferred into the hearts and minds of as many people in the organisation as possible. Fullan (2001) maintains that change is not linear; it has spells of uncertainty, the intrusion of the unexpected. As he puts it

> The challenge is to disturb the organisations in a manner that approximates the desired outcomes.

Whatever else one can say, it is sure to be complex, though interesting. In the process of change, according to Fullan, there are six issues to be aware of

- The goal is not to innovate the most

He makes a difference between innovation and innovativeness, a subtle distinction perhaps, but implying that transformational leaders do not think of ideas for the sake of making change, rather they creatively produce concepts and actions that will help bring the change about. Wise leaders decide on the innovation likely to make transformational impact and work with that until it happens.

- It is not enough to have the best ideas

A variety of skills are needed in truly transformational teams. One is to have a person in the team who is a completer-finisher, otherwise great ideas disappear, lost forever. And having good ideas is not much use if people cannot be persuaded to buy into them. The best ideas are those addressing needs that are sensed and facts that should be faced, put together by a committed team who have a deep moral purpose motivating their activity. Bright ideas are best when there is something *behind* them; and some attraction *ahead* if they are successful.

- Appreciate the implementation dip

It would be nice to think that new ideas were immediately embedded and blossomed; like newly placed plants in a garden they take a while to come to bloom. Discouragement can be warded off if there is understanding that sometimes movement is backward for a bit before things go forward.

- Redefine resistance

All new ideas seem to have some resistors and detractors: to the single-minded visionary they can be frustrating and annoying. Fullan reckons that there is more to be learned from those with whom we disagree than from those whose opinions we share.

It must be true. In my days as a mathematics teacher, I used to try to persuade students that they learned more from correcting wrong answers than from getting everything right. They were not persuaded; they liked ticks on their work, I like approval too. I still believe I was right, and I think Fullan is too. It requires a different mind set about objection and resistance.

Heifetz and Linsky (2002) have done research into why resistance happens. They believe that there are two types of change, technical change and adaptive change, the former rather more easily handled than the latter. Technical change would include improving literacy and numeracy, for example: adaptive change is transformation of the system. In the researchers' view

Adaptive change stimulates resistance because it challenges people's habits, beliefs and values. It asks them to take a loss, experience uncertainty, and even express disloyalty to people and cultures. Because adaptive change forces people to question and perhaps redefine aspects of their identity, it also challenges their sense of competence. Loss, disloyalty, and feeling incompetent: that's a lot to ask. No wonder people resist.

It is as well to understand this process so that communication can be sensitive and productive. Blundering in with an expectation that people will surrender much of what they once believed is as naïve as it is unrealistic. However, ways and means have to be devised to make it possible, otherwise you will have the map but be unable to make the journey.

- Reculturing is the name of the game

Transformational change is about changing the way people think and behave, so that what once was accepted practice is replaced by something different. The absorption of such changes into behaviour across the whole organisation is what transformational leaders are trying to bring about. That is a complex business and not likely to be linear. It is complex because organisations are made up of people coming from different perspectives: heavy emotion can be involved too. Allies who line up happily behind a new idea evoke pleasure and contentment; resistors create annoyance and frustration unless they are understood. Heifetz and Linsky (2002) delved into this contentious issue too:

People who oppose what you are trying to accomplish are usually those with the most to lose by your success. In contrast, your allies have the least to lose. For opponents to turn around will cost them dearly in terms of disloyalty to their own roots and constituency; for your allies to come along may cost nothing. For that reason, your opponents deserve more of your attention, as a matter of compassion, as well as a tactic of strategy and survival.

Situations of this kind are apparent in politics and also in schools. Guided by the wisdom of the experienced I changed little when I first took up headship. There were, however, two matters that from the start I could not live with. I inherited a school that was streamed, with no transfer from the sink to the elite. The tutor groups were labelled CAMB and RIDGE; it is not hard to guess where the top sets were. It had been like this for many years, change being resisted particularly by those whose subjects appeared only in the CAMB stream so that they were rarely exposed to the students generally regarded as more challenging. Change had to happen whether they agreed or not. In the best scenario the old guard can be won round from their position where they perceive they will be losers: this will only be achieved if their arguments, and personal consequences, are understood and appreciated. Changing systems or structures so that power bases are affected will meet some resistance for reasons that Heifetz and Linsky so lucidly explain.

One of the wonderful graces of Nelson Mandela is his willingness to understand and apply this principle. He realised that others had much to lose if he was to see the triumph of his ideas. The wisdom with which Mandela handled De Klerk contributed to a transformation that did not prove to be the expected bloodbath.

• Never a checklist, always complexity

The best teaching enables students to apply lessons learned and principles taught to a wide variety of contexts. Sometimes teachers resort, for understandable reasons, to teaching to

the examination paper, a process often meaning that unless a student is faced with an identical question to one they have done before there is confusion. But life is rarely like that so principles are more important than quick fixes. The principles that are being proposed here are not quick fix solutions but processes through which transformational change necessarily has to pass, almost always in the order that is presented in this book.

Having created a practical vision, it is necessary for the team to **help others to believe** in it. This will present a challenge to some staff in most organisations.

After years of instability, incremental change or failed attempts at change, staff can internalise a deep belief that they are not capable of achieving a leap was how John Kotter put it. His advice was clear enough: *If your people do not have experience with significant successful change, make sure you find credible sources and have them constantly available.*

When vision is introduced it may be met with a stunned silence. When Marie Stubbs outlined her hopes to staff at her new school she said there was 'a trapped, wary feeling in the room'. She pressed on regardless. 'I'm probably far too old to be doing this kind of thing,' she said, 'so I hope you will be nice to me'. It was meant to raise a smile, but was greeted by total silence. She confessed, 'I suppose there was some childish part of me hoping I would be greeted with open arms': instead she 'felt as welcome as a traffic warden'.

This is an illustration of what Collins and Porras (1995) call the 'Gulp Factor'. 'When it dawns on people what it will take to achieve the vision, there is an almost audible gulp'. The leader's job is to help others believe and this may take time.

These are straightforward practical steps that can make á difference for some for

What good communication should achieve:
address anxieties
modify and harness emotion
sound reasonable
evoke faith

whom change is threatening. Helping staff to believe in themselves as well as the vision benefits everybody.

The most enduring change is based on a persuasion process dealing with **hearts and minds**. Occasionally, that process is by-passed for one reason or another. At a conference dealing with a new initiative from the Department for Education and Skills, one key-note speaker explained that persuading people of the need for action, and the quality of the action proposed would have been desirable but that there simply was not the time: action needed to happen sooner than convincing hearts and minds would allow. This was during what has been described as the era of 'informed prescription': somebody else knows better and they are telling you what to do. It is rarely a good idea and it ought to be avoided wherever possible. Transformational change succeeds best when people are truly 'on board'.

The appearance of a school has great significance. If the environment is a mess so might be the behaviour of the students having to live in it. Criminologists James Wilson and George Kelling introduced what they called the Broken Window theory, arguing that crime is the inevitable result of disorder; at a simple level that is why it is best to remove graffiti in a school the day it is discovered; graffiti has a reproduction cycle faster than rabbits. In Malcolm Gladwell's excellent book *The Tipping Point* (2000) he argues that context is

more powerful than predisposition. In order to create an ethos where young people were treated like students, Nunthorpe School decided to buy lockers for every student and to insist that thereafter no students would be allowed to carry a bag around with them. This decision was not unilaterally declared: indeed, the decision itself was reached only after full discussion of reasons why the proposal was being made were put to the students and parents themselves. Hearts and minds were so won over that the parents agreed to pay a rental for the lockers. This did dramatically change the ethos and played a significant part in the transformation of academic achievement.

Do not underestimate the value of convincing both hearts and minds

Central to this phase is the **art of communication**.

Communication can be so confusing. Students play Chinese whispers to demonstrate it; adults choose often to assume that what they have said, others will have heard. It is not so. In recent years, I came across two masterpieces of miscommunication: A sign in a Japanese hotel informed guests, 'you are invited to take advantage of the chambermaid'; a notice in a Rome laundry offered, 'Ladies, leave your clothes here and spend the afternoon having a good time'. Both were innocent, well-intentioned communications distorted in translation. Leaders can make no such plea and need to be aware and careful. You could be excused for thinking that *leadership-speak* in some schools is like a second language: it might as well be for the impact it has.

The first need for communication is to **allay fear, reduce anxiety**. If positive emotional commitment can be encouraged so much the better. It will have to sound commonsense and must leave many, if not quite all, people feeling that they believe in the transformational agenda proposed through the vision statement. Laurie Beth Jones (1995) observed that

> Leaders intent upon accomplishing anything worthwhile have to enrol others in their cause. Too many have staffs employed on paper but not emotionally enrolled in mission.

Anxiety and fear reduce enrolment. Jesse Jackson wisely commented that the leader's role is not to take sides (with those who are supportive and positively engaged) but to bring all sides together: that takes great skill in communication.

How some staff might feel reminds me of the little boy who was told by his father to stand up: three times he had to be told before he was dragged to his feet, Foolishly, he told his father he was 'still sitting down inside'. Plenty of staff rooms have people in them still sitting down inside. The power of logic and rationale will not always move them. When I was a boy, one of the first books I was able to read had a fable about the sun and the wind having an argument about who could get the coat off the back of a man. The tale told of the extraordinary efforts of the wind before, out of breath, he conceded he could not blow the coat off. The sun did not use force, it warmed it off in no time. Educational leadership has long been a man's world, maybe that is why the rational logical emphasis has been so predominant: but things are changing, and Goleman and others are opening eyes to the coercive power of the sun.

In his book *The Six Dimensions of Leadership* (1999), Andrew Brown develops the concept that most leaders are like actors. He explains that the business of actors involves skilled communication and he cites four areas of skill.

Poets
Rehetoricians
Storytellers
Showmen

Poets, he claims, are those who frame convincing images for their subordinates; rhetoricians energise their audience through their language; storytellers focus, illustrate, celebrate and amplify the feats and beliefs of others; showmen dramatise and explain through action.

All this work of developing skilful communication has, as a central purpose, to make a **strong emotional impact**; action is not only to do with rationality. Leaders would like to build confidence and excitement, generate a feel good factor and yet at the same time behave in a way that is appropriate to the history and culture of the organisation. If the point of communication is to change behaviour, thinking, feeling and commitment, it deserves to be taken far more seriously than it is. At the introduction of Local Management of Schools (LMS), many headteachers went to great lengths to develop the skills required to manage the school finances. Leadership requires excellent communication skills. I know of no headteachers who have explicitly undertaken training to develop these highly prized skills. Once you have mastered LMS the only problem left is balancing the books: training oneself to handle sensitive, changing, vulnerable, difficult, inconsistent and unpredictable people is so much harder: it is a labour that is never finished.

The central purpose of communication is to unleash the real power of the vision because most of those involved **have belief**, a common understanding of goals

Communication is about what I say; what they hear; what we do.

and directions, and become committed to it. Jack Welch had a stammer as a child so learned to communicate in a variety of stimulating ways but always with the foundational belief that *the greatest success comes only when you focus your staff on what really matters.*

Classroom teachers explain what they are communicating in a variety of ways. They give up the idea that you say something once and the whole class will absorb it. Teachers increasingly use multiple intelligence theory to determine how they communicate; how people learn is now recognised as being as important as how teachers teach. Somehow this message seems to have by-passed the communication style of some headteachers who have not realised that staff rooms are mixed ability environments every bit as much as classrooms, and that the people sitting there learn best with a range of different stimuli. We need to become a little wiser in the art of spoken communication.

Communication that counts
- takes time to hone communication skills
- recognises that staff rooms are mixed ability environments
- uses a variety of styles to reflect hearing preferences
- reads audience needs
- emphasises personal communication
- checks carefully that what was said is what was heard
- restricts length of communication appropriately
- emphasises impact at the expense of detail
- recognises that body language speaks loudly
- devises ways to attract attention at the start
- arranges furniture to maximise potential for impact
- appeals to heart and mind
- tells the story
- focuses on positives and actions
- prepares in advance what to say and how to say it
- learns to be flexible and responsive to audience

Keeping the vision fresh in the mind is necessary too. The launch of the vision is often a stimulating and exciting period in transformational change; unless it is kept fresh over the succeeding months

Emphasise Moral Purpose constantly

Celebrate Success generously

the transformation will flag and stall. On a hot and sultry day, when the wind is still and the atmosphere heavy, we open two windows in our house; we know which are best because we have discovered that two of them are so located that the wind blows through, even on the stillest of days, keeping the house fresh.

When the brightness of the initial launch fades, the staff become preoccupied with their own routines, energy levels diminish and impetus slows, then the wind needs to blow through. Celebration and a re-emphasis on why we are all involved helps: they are the windows to be opened so the breeze will blow through the organisation and keep transformation fresh and vibrant. Staleness must not be permitted.

Most human beings have two key instincts that are useful in addressing this issue.

- The first is that people like to feel they have a purpose, that they belong to something bigger to which they make a valid contribution.

- The other is that most people like to be part of some successful activity and to see their work recognised and applauded.

For many, this is much more important than financial reward. I have always been amused by young people's desire to be on camera; they can be part of a football crowd and spend a couple of hours waiting to see a fleeting glimpse of themselves on the television. Adults are much more coy about it but still like to be seen and appreciated. Wise leaders know their staff well enough to know what style of celebration will suit the personal taste of their staff but something will and, properly used, will not only freshen up that person but many of their friends and associates who bask in reflected glory. These are powerful tools in keeping change fresh.

Once launched, the vision needs to be translated into an action plan. This is the next stage in transitional change.

SCHOOL SNAPSHOT

THE SCHOOL Rawcliffe Infant and Nursery School, York
Headteacher: Nick Long
Infant and Nursery, 272 on roll, 5% on Free School Meals, rising roll up from 70 to 90 per year

THE STARTING POINT
September 2000
Parents had little faith in the school as an organisation

The curriculum offered too little opportunity for flexibility or creativity

THE TRANSFORMATION SOUGHT
To free up time for less formal subjects like Music or Technology foundation subjects were forced into slots with no cross-curricular planning

WHAT WAS DONE?
Introduction of a 10 day cycle, discussed with staff

In the cycle, every tenth day became a 'different' day

Met staff to ask how they could contribute to the plan, and agreed about their contributions

Tight objectives were introduced and were shared with staff

These objectives were used in review of progress

Two-way questioning was involved: the head was asked questions on a systematic basis to establish clarity; the staff were asked questions about the progress of their agreed contributions

Celebration became part of this initiative: ' I told as many within the school community as I could, and as often as I could'

Staff were given delegated authority to hold budgets to address agreed targets

Discussion on short-term targets revealed those falling short

Financial support was given to support areas not yet meeting targets, where appropriate

A Star of the Week was nominated and their story told, so placing genuine value on achievement

OUTCOMES
The Tenth Day has become part of the school community's culture

Teachers have become liberated and enthused

Children's learning has advanced considerably

WAS IT WORTH IT?
Yes, because the school has become a better place to learn all subjects across the curriculum

QUOTES
'Please hurry up and finish the register – it's the tenth day'- Nathan, Year 1

SCHOOL SNAPSHOT

THE SCHOOL St. George's R.C. School, Maida Vale, London Headteacher: Lady Marie Stubbs 2000-2001

11-16 comprehensive, 35 staff, 52 languages spoken by students

THE STARTING POINT
March 2000

School placed in Special Measures by Ofsted. It is 'at the bottom end of limited progress'

Literacy and Special Needs are described as 'poor'

'Severe problems with attendance' which is 70%

'Only 20% of the teaching is good', bullying and fighting are rife

Timekeeping is a major cause of concern The role is falling seriously

Academic achievement very low

THE TRANSFORMATION SOUGHT

To take the school out of Special Measures To give staff and students back their dignity and self esteem. To deal with all the issues that were problems at the start

WHAT WAS DONE?

Restrict anxieties to the senior team: Stopped staff calling students 'kids'

Introduce a leaving ball as a 'rite of passage' to give students something to look forward to and talked about the principles to staff. Initially they were not persuaded

Challenge staff position on this issue, told staff what I believe 'our obligations are'

Meet each student individually. Speak in positives, and with a smile

Insist on appropriate dress by staff and students to signal we are a team

Repeat the same messages consistently, eg. 'Don't run'

Emphasise moral purpose, that the students are valued, so are staff – these children 'deserve the best'

Repeat that 'every child is unique and we respect your uniqueness'

Install technology to convey positive messages for all

Tell them they can be successful and import 'stars' to tell them the same; e.g. Kevin Keegan

Consult students on what could be better, and try to do it. Introduce Suggestion Box

Demonstrate picturesquely (give each student an alarm and show them how to use it through drama)

Approach families by letter and in person and leave upbeat message with them

No sarcasm allowed in communication, be positive and 'never humiliate a student'

Display supportive letters about students to staff and students as exemplars of good behaviour

Start the term by publicly and openly greeting students personally and with 'Welcome back!' posters. Make explicit where the school is going: 'This is the year we get off Special Measures'

Share success and make much of it: 'Attendance now 89%; only 1% to go to be normal!'

Remind staff when things are going well to keep going. Don't take eye off the ball

OUTCOMES

Ofsted (2001): 'You have transformed this school' – out of Special Measures

Attendance over 90%, 140 applications for 120 places available

Ofsted recommended the school as a national example of good practice (2001)

WAS IT WORTH IT?

The head said 'I just can't tell you how much this means to me'

QUOTES

'Five terms is not enough to bring about really deep change – that takes about five years'

Ofsted: 'success depended on a strict, positive regime with clear expectations, grounded on a strong set of values and relentless vigour in implementation'

Chapter 8
Have the Plan

Dreams never hurt anybody if you keep working right behind the dreams to make as much of them become real as you can.
Frank W Woolworth

Schools have plans for everything; though how often they are used or remembered is another story. A plan is not to be stored in a draw or filing cabinet; a plan is not to be considered once a year; a plan is not for governors' consumption only; a plan is not to keep Ofsted at bay. A plan is the outcome of considered thought by a team formed in response to needs that are sensed and facts that have been faced. It is based on a vision, clearly and picturesquely communicated, and incorporates ideas that will help to lead to transformation, regardless of where the ideas came from. It is a working document, subject to change as events unfold: it is a vital document. A well-written plan will play a huge part in transformational change.

The process of creating the plan
The vision reveals what it is intended to do; the plan gives an outline of how it is going to be done or, to change the image, the route map shows where we are intending to go, the plan reveals the means of travel and the path we are going to take. Richard Branson says that plans need to be three things:

> **Related to the core purpose**
> **Fun**
> **Challenging**

In his autobiography Branson (2002) outlines his broad philosophy in the simplest of terms,

> However tight things are, you still need to have the big picture in the front of your mind.

The big picture for him, his Moral Purpose, was *all about service, value for money and offering a simple product.*

The transformational plan in any organisation has to be based on, and constantly refer to, the big picture. Branson's driving purpose may be different in nature to the educational conviction that drives us but it is a moral purpose just the same.

Most plans I have seen could hardly be described as fun, yet the notion that people enjoy working with the plan is a wonderful ambition. Plans that catch the imagination, that have outcomes that are destined to be rewarding and satisfying, are the plans that will lead to significant change. Plans enabling people to enjoy their work and to realise they are enjoying it is an important part of leadership. Something of the showman helped Branson in that. Being ever imaginative, he became regarded as a self-publicist. However, what seems to be true is that his outlandish publicity brought an immense sense of spirit and fun to his employees, who seemed prepared to give everything to the fulfilment of the vision. It was immensely successful. Discovering our own ways to energise the staff in our institutions by creating a plan that has life, vitality, stimulating activity and great hope is essential to transforming vision into dynamic change. Plans in themselves rarely create life but they can be remarkably effective at stifling it.

Those who know Branson's history will not be surprised that he regards challenge as a vital ingredient in plans that bring transformation. Ever seeking the personal challenge, he brought the same attitude to his enterprises. People thrive on challenge. John Steinbeck believed that *people need responsibility. They resist assuming it, but they cannot get along without it.*

Though clearly a generalisation, this is profound truth. Responsibility and challenge often go together, and, though people grumble occasionally about 'extra responsibility', they almost always value it, feel encouraged and liberated by it, and rise to meet it. Plans with potential for making great change will include the element of challenge. Fullan (2001) says that for more radical change,

> The organisation needs leadership that welcomes differences, communicates the urgency of the challenge, talks about broad possibilities in an exciting way, and creates mechanisms that motivate people to reach beyond themselves.

It is all there: fun and challenge. To go beyond whatever was thought possible you have to help people to *believe* they can make it happen.

It is rarely beneficial for a leader to write the plan alone. Far better is to write it along with different groups of people. Finding time to think clearly about all possibilities is essential too. One mechanism is to create small groups to consider issues and prepare presentations rather than dealing with the issues only in the leadership team. Edward de Bono (1999) has some brilliantly imaginative ideas on how to draw creative thinking out of colleagues. De Bono argues that there are a range of thinking processes that need to be drawn out in order to discover the best plans for action. He illustrates these by coloured hats, and even suggests that in major board meetings in corporations across the world people put the hats on! I have never done that but I have introduced the theory in planning meetings in my school to discern the right road ahead.

The hats are not magic, but the process can be really helpful. De Bono argues that many hours are wasted in meetings because thinking is not clear, does not easily reach conclusions, generates unnecessary heat and is uneconomic. His process involves isolating the thinking styles taking place in the dialogue so that maximum benefit is derived. I have found this helpful in devising plans; for example when people are being imaginative and creative with ideas, someone inevitably raises an objection which will have two effects: it lengthens the debate but even more importantly it deters others from offering their view. They think they are going to face objectors as soon as they open their mouths, so limiting the areas into which dialogue may wander is beneficial, economic and constructive. It helps to inhibit damaging negative talk by referring to practical disciplines of procedure rather than putting someone down personally or permitting the damage they might do and the time they waste. It is a discipline of practice.

The green hat approach threw up the idea of private tuition. It began with a simple question, 'If we had £50 000 what ideas can we think of that would guarantee improved academic performance at Key Stage 4?' No one was allowed to comment on any suggestion until they had all been heard. There were eight or nine ideas: two emerged as 'catching the imagination' and were translated into action in school.

White hat: facts and fugures
Red hat: emotions and feelings
Black hat: caution and care
Yellow hat: speculation and positive judgement
Green hat: creativity
Blue hat: observation and overview

As far as the process is concerned, De Bono's summary rings bells with me: *There is nothing more sad and wasteful than a roomful of intelligent and highly paid people waiting for a chance to attack something the speaker has said.*

It happens all the time; it is wasteful and it is sad; it is also counterproductive. There has to be a better way, and it is important to find it.

Once the process is agreed and undertaken, what needs to be in the plan?

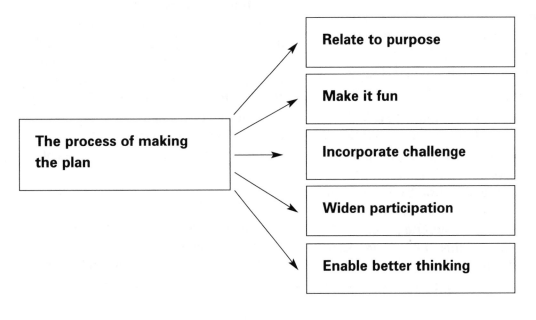

Targets and outcomes

It is important that a document emerges out of all the creative thinking that is relatively brief, clear and specific and sets measurable targets. One of the problems that arise from performance reviews can be difference of opinion about the performance itself. Almost always, this harks back to unclear, vague expectations defined in previous reviews. The review itself is straightforward if the targets and outcomes were clear enough at the start. I have always worked on the notion that teachers ought to be able to know how well they have done against their agreed targets *before* they meet to discuss it with anybody. It is a sure sign that targets should have been better prepared if you enter into a dispute about performance.

The best targets in plans are challenging but realistic; they have responsibility built into them, with authority delegated along with the responsibility to empower the member of staff to meet the targets and have timescales that are manageable. General Patton, American soldier and leader, believed that it is best *never to tell people how to do things. Tell them what you want them to achieve and they will surprise you by their ingenuity.*

And they will enjoy doing it.

Funding

There is never going to be enough money! Any leader who cannot think beyond what is affordable is unimaginative, but then it is like that at home too. It is the same everywhere.

The costs of plans should be calculated and funding should be allocated proportionate to the demands of the plan. Frustration arises whenever initiatives are to be undertaken without adequate funding. This will mean prioritising. The vision has to be paramount and this makes it necessary to make hard choices. If the vision is not seen as the priority for funding, then it

will not transform anything, because it has been strangled at birth.

If the vision is for transformation of uses of new technology in Key Stage 2, then it may have to be that money for furniture and books is sacrificed. The plan has to prioritise the vision or it will not transform.

Visions that cannot be afforded should not be undertaken because they will precipitate a cycle of failure that will breed suspicion about future initiatives. It is better to wait if it is impossible to generate enough funding to support the transformation. The 'It's them, not us' syndrome is a serious threat here; it is easy to blame the government or the council or whoever 'they' are. Such blame achieves nothing. I know it is a problem (I can say that with confidence; my school's budget has been dreadful for years) but I prefer to see leaders taking control of their own circumstances. Long ago, George Bernhard Shaw shared this wisdom:

> People are always blaming their circumstances. I don't believe in circumstances. The people who get on in this world are the people who get up and look for the circumstances they want and, if they can't find them, make them.

Involving others

The creation of the plan involved significant others, and yet there are often many more employees still to become engaged in the transformational plan. Briefing them will require all the skills of communication discussed in chapter 6 and 7. The wider the feeling of involvement the better the chances of success.

Kotter believes that

> Major internal transformation rarely happens unless many people assist. Yet employees generally won't help, or can't help, if they feel relatively

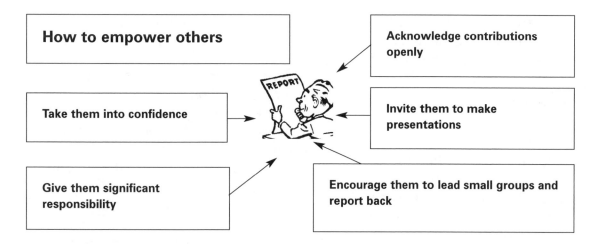

powerless; hence the relevance of empowerment.

Empowerment has become the politically correct mantra of our times. Ever the realist, Kotter recognises this as a potential problem but concludes

> I am not enthusiastic about using faddish words, but in this ever faster-moving world, I think the idea of helping more people to become more powerful is important.

• Take them into your confidence

People like to feel as though they know things; if they are trusted, most people rise to the level of trust though just occasionally they will not and different strategies have to be used. It must be genuine as falseness is easily seen through and will rebound on the leaders who demonstrate it. Taking people into your confidence may be done in groups, for example by revealing that something has really disturbed your equanimity or individually, when it is powerful because it feels much more special. What it does is lead to engagement with the plan, a personal involvement and commitment that can only be beneficial and it opens up opportunity for listening for new ideas and provides personal support to leaders too. Though it is threatening for some people if notes are taken during conversation, it is wise to record good ideas and suggestions, so long as colleagues know that is what you are

doing. They may even be flattered. Richard Branson was noted for always having a standard school pad with him which he called his 'most essential possession'. What did he use it for?

> I write down all the comments I hear from Virgin staff and anyone else I meet. The discipline of writing everything down means I really listen to people.

Recently I told a colleague that I was worried that I would be unable to find a teacher of Religious Studies because the vacancy arose the day before holiday, making it almost impossible for anyone to hand in notice in time for the resignation deadline. I took the colleague into my confidence at 12.45 pm. At 2 pm he came to see me saying he had rung his wife who knew someone in Leeds who had applied for a post at her school but had been unable to come for interview. He had no idea how good she was but he passed her name on anyway. At 7.30 pm she was appointed at my school. My colleague felt good about that, so did I and so did she. People like to be involved.

• Give them significant responsibility

Transformational leaders know that they cannot make change on their own. Significant responsibility has really to mean significant. When people realise that the success of the enterprise depends on them, staff respond; no one wants to feel that their contribution is simply to make up the numbers. If they are treated like spare parts, they will behave accordingly.

When writing the plan, care needs to be taken about who as well as what. When people realise that they were a forethought not an afterthought and that they were planned into a role within the whole plan, they commit in powerful ways. Sometimes it is risky and leaders are not foolhardy, but risk-taking can pay huge dividends. Much as I dislike the idea, poachers do occasionally make splendid gamekeepers.

• Invite them to make presentations

Leaders are meant to lead, but not in everything. One of the most powerful ways of giving responsibility is to trust people to say what you might have said; to present the case for aspects of the change. Fine decisions have to be made here, but the outcomes should be considered. More people might be influenced if ideas shared by the leader are actually presented by someone else. Moreover, using another person will cause them to grow and be engaged far more dramatically. Certainly presenting plans and programmes to others raises self-esteem and status, both of which involve emotional engagement with the transformational change. If leaders have problems with being 'the actor', this opportunity may help to solve the problem. There are some very skilled people amongst our employees waiting to be released.

At the time of the introduction of threshold payments for teachers satisfying eight criteria, there was potential for serious conflict between staff and leadership. We decided to work closely with the unions and to invite them to present our agreed conclusions to the whole staff. This calculated risk paid off handsomely with a most smooth implementation of an otherwise contentious initiative. It does not always work but the risk is worth calculating.

• Encourage people to lead small groups and report back

Not everybody is comfortable making presentations, either in leadership or amongst the staff but most are capable of, and enjoy, leading small groups. In transformational change in my school, I have asked staff from across the various levels of responsibility to lead small groups. This meant, on occasion, newly qualified teachers leading a group including senior teachers. It has never been a problem but rather liberating and encouraging. The requirement to report back adds gravitas to the proceedings, and status to the activity and it can be extremely helpful.

Tom Farmer, founder of Kwik-Fit, applied this principle in his successful transformation of his company:

> The real art of delegation is to be able to give people responsibility, give them authority, but also make them accountable, and ensure there is a very good report back system to the leader.

• Acknowledge contributions openly

Those who have performed well when given responsibility need to be acknowledged. The wider and more open the acknowledgement the better. If governors are informed or parents notified when someone else's good idea is implemented, it has strong motivational influence on the successful introduction of the plan.

Single mindedness

It is important that the plan is not part of too many plans. It needs to have a clear place all its own at the top of the agenda. J K Galbraith wrote, '*According to the experience of all but the most accomplished jugglers, it is easier to keep one ball in the air than many*'. That is certainly true about making the plan;

watering its importance down by mingling the transformational agenda with others will result in failure. The plan has to be top of the agenda. This involves three actions:

- **Make it attractive to be involved with the plan**

- **Make it difficult to drift away from the plan**

- **Make it impossible to miss the significant of the plan**

It will be attractive if those involved draw the attention of colleagues to it, receive the acknowledgement of leadership, are seen to be rewarded for their involvement, feel and are seen to feel fulfilled by their involvement and have their story told on appropriate and significant occasions.

Alongside making the plan attractive, it will be necessary to make reversion to old ways difficult or less attractive. Those who resist will initially keep quiet in the hope that the phase will pass – then they will attempt to revert back to the old ways.

If, for example, the transformation is to do with Teaching and Learning, some will embrace the vision and the plan openly, some will learn quickly and move with the initiative, changing approaches confidently, but some will slip back into past practice and take others with them. This must be challenged.

If the plan is constantly exposed, it will be a challenge in itself. Transformational leaders repeat the ideas in the plan, introduce them in a variety of different forums such as staff meetings, at Professional Development Days, on the agendas of departmental meetings, with parents etc. Repeating the statement of transformational vision again and again, preferably in a variety of ways, is the only way to ensure that it is being heard and heard correctly.

Difficulties

Fullan (2001) reminded us that not everything will run smoothly, calling this complexity science. Branson gave a typical example of establishing a mail-order company that was heading to lead the way but depended on the post. Out of the blue, just at the wrong time, came the announcement of a sixth-month postal strike! It was a case of re-inventing themselves or going bust.

All plans face challenges: an unexpected reduction in budget, the promotion of a key member of staff, a new initiative from government that adds to the workload or the illness of key people. There has to be flexibility; the eye has daily to be on the ball.

As an *aide-memoire*, John Maxwell (1998), chose an acrostic to chart the course of planning.

P	**Predetermine a course of action**
L	**Lay out your goals**
A	**Adjust your priorities**
N	**Notify key personnel**
A	**Allow time for acceptance**
H	**Head into action**
E	**Expect problems**
A	**Always point to successes**
D	**Daily review your plan**

That is the plan, but how do you make it happen?

SCHOOL SNAPSHOT

THE SCHOOL Whale Hill Primary School, Middlesbrough Headteacher: Norma Newell

Roll 508 including 78 part-time nursery children

Free school meals 39%, 23 teachers, 15 classroom assistants

THE STARTING POINT

Standards in the core subjects were lower than they ought to be (Ofsted 2002)

Staff were 'working their socks off' but these standards were still too low

THE TRANSFORMATION SOUGHT

To raise these standards clearly and significantly

THE PLAN MADE:

The team leading the school worked with staff to agree a plan of action

New responsibilities were put in place – the right people were selected to lead the change effort

New approaches were piloted and new initiatives introduced

All new initiatives were related back to moral purpose, at each stage

A pre-school 'mental-maths club' each day was started by staff (nearly 300 children attended) for 15 minutes

Staff started teaching earlier thus extending voluntarily their working day

Greater emphasis placed on 'making pupils' progress more picturesque' (Rowling 2002)

'Traffic Light system' introduced to clearly show progress of children with writing

Moral Purpose was writ large in all these activities; it was repeated again and again

OUTCOMES

KS 2 teacher assessments show satisfying improvements

The school has a strengthened corporate moral purpose amongst all staff, whether teachers or support staff

WAS IT WORTH IT?

The actions have 'intensified our sense of professional vocation – the sheer joy of a job well done'

QUOTES

As a school we 'feel relentlessly positive with a new release of energy and vitality'

SCHOOL SNAPSHOT

THE SCHOOL Longbenton Community College
Principal: Jim Cockburn

11-18 Community College, Technology Specialism, 900 on roll, free school meals 21%, 47% 5 A* to C, 60 staff

THE STARTING POINT

The College Sixth Form was not large, some courses struggling for viability. A recurring theme of two Ofsted Inspections had been concerns about future viability. The advent of the Learning and Skills Council posed another threat

THE TRANSFORMATION SOUGHT

To increase participation in post 16 education, including a widening of choice, through a collaborative programme with two other colleges

THE PLAN MADE:

The concept 'began small', as a pilot project

Three courses were offered using video conferencing shared by the three colleges. After two years further courses were offered

A collaborative framework was designed by the three principals, involving a mixture of video conferencing as well as shared opportunity to offer courses on separate bases, so that students travelled between colleges to access provision

Staff worked collaboratively to prepare courses and in sharing of resources

OUTCOMES

Each college has increased numbers and strengthened provision

Wider ranges of courses were available to students within relatively close proximity to their colleges

Staff benefited greatly from collaborative working particularly sharing of ideas and resources

The actual results of our students placed us second in our Borough in 2002 in terms of achievement at post 16 level

WAS IT WORTH IT?

'Yes, it was. I believe there is need to retain quality sixth form provision on this site. This collaborative worked well to deliver opportunity that our students have valued. We were delighted with what they achieved last year.'

QUOTES

'Our colleges have come to trust each other. Collaboration has been good for all involved and has worked really well.'

Chapter 9
Making it happen

The best thought-out plans in the world are not worth the paper they are written on if you can't pull them off.
Ralph Larsen

Ralph Larsen, Chairman and CEO of Johnson and Johnson (2002) talked about *pulling it off* or *making it happen*. This is the focus of transformational change. Making it happen suits me better because it sounds as though it is the result of conscious action; pulling it off sounds lucky. Bossidy and Charan called their book *Execution: the Discipline of Getting Things Done* (2002). It was grim enough to attract my attention, but I soon discovered that for them it is grimly serious because, unless leaders and their fellow workers get things done, a gap is left between what an organisation's leaders wanted to achieve and their ability to deliver it. If leaders take execution seriously they make sure that what they want to achieve is challenging but also achievable. If execution is so important there is little sense in setting oneself up to fail.

Bossidy reckons that by custom and practice many leaders regard execution as detail work that is beneath their dignity. However, in his view it is a leader's *most important job* and so it should be because no matter how creatively clever the plan contrived, failure to execute it signals only that a person's aspirations were greater than their ability to perform. This is not a good message and even more dangerous when carried into the collective memory.

Charan concluded:

> I saw leaders placing too much emphasis on what some call high-level strategy, on intellectualising and philosophising, and not enough on implementation.
>
> Execution is not just tactics – it is a discipline and a system. It has to be built into an organisation's strategy, goals and culture.

That is a transformational challenge in itself for some organisations, and crucial to success.

When the vision has been created, the plan developed and in place, communication and delegation of responsibility has been passed on to employees and commitment appears high, this is the end of the beginning. There is still a long way to go. Some steps are now suggested to make it happen.

The Making it Happen cycle

There is no formula. Complexity science ensures that spanners will be thrown into collective works at some stage. Nonetheless there are some principles determining a culture that more easily makes things happen. Leaders will be alert to progress, not forever uprooting the developing growth but instead reading the signs at scheduled and regular intervals. Much can be gleaned by skilled analysis.

1. Agree interim targets

Discussion should be undertaken with each team leader until agreement is reached on interim targets lying within the responsibility of that team. Explicit agreement on moral purpose needs to be reached. Once agreed, this should be written down.

2. Check that these targets are passed on

It needs to be understood that the leaders will check that the agreed activities have actually happened. It is important that all team members are as aware as the leader about what has been agreed, and that they are clear about moral purpose. If leaders are able to build a culture where they are reminded if something important is forgotten this will help. Wise leaders make it known when someone reminded them about something they had agreed to do. Selectively revealing a little weakness can be positive and encourage staff.

3. Hold pre-emptive dialogue

Having agreed targets (see 1) it is necessary to have a scheduled meeting to discuss how work is progressing towards the transformational target. People generally like to know someone is taking an interest in what they are doing; that it is important enough for someone to want to know what is going on. Some leaders approach this accountability process with trepidation but all it needs is to be handled with sensitivity and genuine supportive interest, shown by both words and actions.

4. Offer encouragement and support

What leaders will see is significant progress and what is commendable should be commended. Some aspects of the change towards the targets will not be progressing so well. It is reasonable to ask what might be done to help, what the barriers have been and whether there are thoughts about the best way to move back on track.

Black and Gregersen (2002) did a concise but brilliant analysis of why plans fail. They identified three possible stages for failure:

The first was the possibility that the plan was not truly registered with people: this they called

• The Failure to See

Most of us experienced this in class when we were young, and certainly in the classes we have taught: the way of pretending to understand and hoping nobody checks and that *our* ignorance will not become embarrassingly public.

Sometimes people see some of the way but not enough to complete the journey. The sooner one can discover the failure to see, the less embarrassment there will be restoring someone to the right path.

- **The Failure to Move**

Black and Gregeren talk about people being 'immobilised', wanting to move but unable to simply get moving. They attribute this to the fear factor saying that 'many people prefer being competent at the wrong thing than incompetent at the right thing'. Quite what goes through a rabbit's head when it is stuck in the headlights I do not know but it does seem silly to sit and be run over when you could move! Fear does freeze us, and careful, considerate, compassionate support and guidance is essential to create the movement towards embracing change.

- **The Failure to Finish**

People get tired and people get lost, concluded Black and Gregersen. Re-energising, re-engaging the disengaged and re-focusing the lost are as necessary for teachers as they are for the students who fail to finish. Sometimes leaders can be so far ahead of the pack that they forget what is going on behind. Ancient shepherds in the Middle East used to concentrate behind as well as ahead. That is why David explained in Psalm 23 that goodness and mercy followed the sheep. Leaders would do well to employ both in their attempts to help those who are struggling to keep up with the pace.

When I was a young teacher someone said to me that you will need eyes in the back of your head and being a leader requires the same ability to see both ahead and behind.

5. Do not celebrate too soon
While celebrating success it is important to remind the staff of the longer-term plan and that this is a battle won, not the war. This avoids what Kotter calls 'happy talk': it does no harm so long as the team members do not take their eyes off the final goal.

The Sheffield rally organised by the Labour Party under Neil Kinnock was a sad example of celebrating too soon. It was not the rally itself that was the problem, more the perception that there was premature celebration, 'declaring victory before the battle was over'.

6. Schedule report back from teams
After the pre-emptive meeting, team leaders should know there will be a formal scheduled meeting at which a full report of progress towards interim targets will be discussed. All members of the team should have a part to play in constructing the report so that they all own the situation. This will mean all the staff realise how well they are doing, or whether they are falling short. The report should contain some ideas about the way forward, including proposals to get back on track for those who have missed targets. It is important to schedule these meetings in advance so that they are not interpreted as hunting out those who are falling short and ensure that they happen whether there is progress or not.

This process of review will become part of the changing culture of the school. MacBeath and Myers (1999) advised that review and introspection should not occur only when Ofsted knocks on the door but that it should be *extensive, internal and integral to the day to day life of the school*. Probing and thoughtful questions should be asked in the reviewing process.

7. Ask key questions
Jack Welch did not have much time for written reports from his team leaders, preferring instead to meet them on a regular basis. He said,

> Throughout my career, I never wanted to see a 'report' before the person presented it. To me the value of these sessions was not in reports. It was in the heads and hearts of those

reporting. I wanted to drill down, get beyond the reports and into the thinking that went into them.

That is where questioning comes in. Bossidy (2002) says that the asking of questions is a key issue.

> Often a leader is just sociable and courteous. She shows interest in their children (of team leaders) (that's OK); or she chats about baseball (this is America), with a few superficial questions about the business. This leader is not engaged in the business.

Bossidy argues that the team leaders who are

> ...any good will be disappointed by superficiality. They will ask, 'What was the point?' Good leaders like to be quizzed because they know more about their part of the business than the leader; and, of course, the leader has learned very little either.

Questions need to be probing, stretching, challenging. Good questioning will lead to the overall leader being better informed and the team leaders feeling reinforced in what they do and with greater self-confidence and determination about the future.

Secretan (1996) believed that *there are plenty of people with answers, but few with the wisdom to ask the right questions*. It is a skill that can be learned.

8. Readjust targets and focus

Not everything that team leaders planned and hoped will have been achieved; some will have exceeded targets, others will not have reached them. Progress is seldom predictable or linear. It is sensible and reasonable to discuss new targets without instilling a sense of triumphalism or failure. Team leaders need to work out the focus for the next stage so that they can meet targets in the subsequent cycle. Missing targets implies bad target setting or that there is some problem, so adjustments will need to be made.

9. Interject further targeted support

Success or failure is not all to do with funding but a thorough review may reveal the necessity for extra support. If priorities mean anything at all then finding funding to assist in reaching targets associated with them is essential. Support can take many forms not only money but time allocated to the team, more technical assistance or more training of team members on specific transformational issues. It is important that matters are not left too long before a close look is taken with the team leader to ascertain whether progress is being made at the expected rate, and why. It is to help the team to put matters right and to give them cause to feel good and to celebrate success. People feel good when they sense support. This feel-good factor can develop a helpful momentum of its own.

If the transformational effort is to raise boys' achievement and it is known that the boys would perform better in smaller classes, resources have to be found to support the vision: if a year group is perceived to be performing badly it may well need a financial focus. Sensible, specific targeted support is likely to be effective.

10. Agree success and feedback

During the discussion with team leaders it is essential to discover what has been working well, who has contributed significantly and how. Too often these analyses of success can be rushed to make way for the business of diagnosing weakness. This is a great mistake, as significant time must be given to finding out what and who is working well, systematically and thoroughly; cursory acknowledgement of achievement and in depth debate about failure transmits all the wrong messages.

11. Celebrate short-term wins

For short-term wins to have beneficial impact they have to have six characteristics.

Short-Term Wins

- have to be *visible*

- have to be *unmistakeable*

- have to be related to the *change effort*

- have to be *acknowledged*

- have to be kept in *perspective*

- have to be used to *stimulate* others

Visible means that people can see a success and who achieved it and it is better still if they can also see why it was successful. It is important that achievements have an authenticity about them that recognises the workforce. Giving artificial or relatively trivial achievements disproportionate recognition dilutes the power of the short-term win philosophy. Kotter believes it to be important that *large numbers of people can see for themselves that the result is real not just hype.* Credibility is crucial.

Schools have for years rewarded students for effort as well as achievement and it is just as valid to do this for the staff too. People can only be expected to do their best and leaders should recognise that they have.

This is a short-term win strategy, not the celebration of total culture change. However, it is a big step along the way and good cause for celebration and should be used to generate momentum not to slow it. As an executive of Kimberley-Clark said, *I am delighted, but not yet satisfied.* Satisfaction comes at the end of the battle.

Rudolph Guiliani practiced the theory of short-term wins,

> Whenever I started a new endeavour, I looked to have clear, decisive victory as early as I could. It need not have been a large initiative, and in fact it was usually better if the problem was small enough so that it could be easily understood and yielded an

unambiguous solution. This gave people hope. And let constituents, employees and even critics know that action and positive change were more than just rhetoric.

What short-term wins achieve

John Kotter defined short-term wins as: '*Victories that nourish faith in the change effort; emotional rewards for hard workers; holders of critics at bay and momentum builders*'.

The word inspiration is derived from the Latin for breathe in. Leaders who celebrate short-term winners breathe life, hope and expectancy into the work force, saying that our goals are achieveable, we are on the way, we will succeed.

They are rewarders too, who give those practically engaged in the transformational change working towards agreed goals and expending effort in a common cause a pat on the back. They take the opportunity to say two things, Well Done and Thank You. The power of these words should not be underestimated.

Jack Welch made a self-depricating observation about his role when he said

> I might not be the brightest bulb in the chandelier, but over the years, I have always thought I was pretty good at getting most of the bulbs to light up.

Rewards light up people's lives, as does expressed appreciation and the combined light of the bulbs casts much more brightness than one can do on its own.

Most people want to be a winner and like the feeling of being 'part of something special'. Seeing evidence of success encourages the reluctant to become more involved, and challenges the resistant. The least it will do is make it more difficult for the cynic to spread a malign influence.

Short-term wins accelerate the development of change, pushing the movement forward a little to add what Collins calls momentum. It is leaders who develop the vision, recruit commitment and work with others to create a plan. Review is part of the making it happen process revealing conspicuous success and celebrating it. All build up momentum, the feeling that we are onto a good thing and can become unstoppable. This is a powerful stage in transformational change.

It is essential not to mind if others take the credit for something that may have started life as your idea. To aspirational leaders, transformation is more important than who is credited for it. Lao Tzu summarised this aspect of leadership in the familiar words,

> Go to the people
> Live among them
> Start with what they know
> And when the deed is done
> The mission accomplished
> Of the best leaders
> The People will say
> We did it ourselves.

It is easy to say but it takes a big person to do this.

12. Evaluate, amend plan and move forward

Actions do go round in circles. The leaders take time to evaluate progress, to amend the plan and to propose forward movement. The circular process renews commitment through re-engaging emotions, facing new facts, adjusting team structures and memberships, repeating vision and modifying the plan.

The whole transitional change then moves considerably further forward.

If leaders play their part in making transformational change happen, changing the culture of an institution, transforming teaching and learning or modifying behaviour throughout an organisation, they are performing a significant service to the community and truly making a difference. Those who have been part of it will take with them the lessons learned into their own futures, with immeasurable effects.

Kotter saw the value of such work.

> Those leaders at the top of enterprises today who encourage others to leap into the future, who help them overcome natural fears, and who thus expand the leadership capacity in their organisations – these people provide a profoundly important service for the entire human community.

What a service to provide, what a difference to be making, what a privilege to be engaged in transformational change. The challenge is to make a difference today and leave lasting influence.

According to John C Maxwell there are four levels of leadership.

- **Achievement** comes to someone when she is able to do great things herself.

- **Success** comes when she empowers followers to do great things with her.

- **Significance** comes when she develops leaders to do great things for her.

- **Legacy** is created when a person puts her organisation into the position to do great things without her.

For over two years I have been encouraged to think about succession since I have been headteacher in the same school for over nineteen years. Staff ask, 'What will happen when you go?' Thinking about succession is not

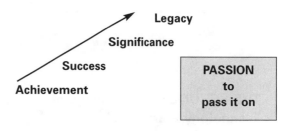

easy because it implies one's own mortality. If our fundamental purpose is to make a difference, it is good to think that the difference might have some permanence. The best leadership moves through an emphasis on personal achievement to wider success in work with others. Significance is achieved when you are able to persuade people to do great things for you but the ultimate is the empowerment of others to do great things when you are no longer around.

Fullan in his latest work (2003) articulated a clear responsibility of leaders:,

> Leadership is crucial to large-scale, sustainable reform. It cuts across all pieces of the change puzzle. It represents the strategy of the twenty-first century. We need pipelines of leadership, leadership at all levels, and opportunity for future and current leaders to learn in context. Above all, we need to cultivate leaders who understand and internalise the underlying conceptions of change and pedagogy, not just the surface terms and leaders. We need leaders who can simultaneously drill down in their own organisations while realising the 'big picture'. The main mark of effective leaders is not how they impact on the bottom line of student achievement at the end of their tenure, but rather, how many effective leaders they cultivate and leave behind who can go even deeper than they did.

Let's go for Legacy!

SCHOOL SNAPSHOT

THE SCHOOL Manor College of Technology, Hartlepool Headteacher: Alan White

11-16 specialist Technology College, 1000 on roll, 21-35% on Free School Meals, 62 staff, 38 % 5 A• to C in 2000

THE STARTING POINT

The school had a declining roll (then standing at 700) and a consequential problem in finances at the time of appointment of the new headteacher in 1996

THE TRANSFORMATION SOUGHT

To create a 'grammar school' ethos with old fashioned values and hi-tech, comprehensive context

To have financial stability, to be over-subscribed, high achieving and well respected in the community for its standards set in uniform, behaviour and extra-curricular activities

HOW DID YOU MAKE IT HAPPEN?

Made people accountable through reviews with SMT line managers three times per year

Developed close checking mechanisms on data to confirm targets were being reached

Focused on staff to deliver change as the most important resource, cutting back capitation to retain that focus when times were hard

Key staff were appointed, and those creating blockages removed or given new challenges

Hard decisions were made when more senior staff in post were not believed to be as effective as less senior alternatives

Serious (sometimes awesome) responsibility given to staff, with support and accountability built in

A 'questioning culture' was developed where sharp questions were posed and anticipated

External assessment and monitoring was invited, evaluated and used to make amendments to plans

Senior leadership team members took delegated responsibility for sub-sections of staff engaged on the transformation agenda, reporting back findings to full SMT to ensure that targets were being met

A range of rewards was introduced to serve as acknowledgements of, and also incentives to, staff

OUTCOMES

The school has achieved specialist Technology College status, is heavily over-subscribed, has developed countless extra-curricular activities, is a Football Foundation Centre and is a Yamaha Music School. Record exam results at both Key Stages. Ofsted (Jan 2000) reported that Manor was 'an effective College with no key issues for action.'

WAS IT WORTH IT?

Yes. The self-fulfilling feel-good factor has developed strongly and impacts on the work of the College

QUOTES

'He who pursues two hares catches neither – define your mission and stick to it.'

Chapter 10

Knowing where to put your weight

He is a wise man who wastes no energy on pursuits for which he is not fitted; and he is wiser still who from among things he can do well, chooses and resolutely follows the best.
William Gladstone

I was brought up in a football belt – rugby was not mentioned, except with disdain. Imagine then the frustration of acquiring a first teaching post in a rugby-playing school where the opposite philosophy applied. Because I was sport obsessed, I decided to engage wholly with the new sport and was soon offered the opportunity of coaching a junior team. I had a good mentor because the Head of Physical Education was the England rugby coach at the time. One day as we were watching a senior match together, I marvelled at how well one of the forwards was playing, not a huge man but an impressive performer. I asked the England man what he thought made him so good and he replied 'if you watch closely he knows exactly where to put his weight'. This was a player who knew where to apply his effort to make the difference, a great skill and one I long since realised that I need too.

The conditions in which transformation is possible have been expressed in a mathematical equation by R Jacobs (1994):

C=A*B*D>X
where
C is the probability of change being successful
A is the dissatisfaction with the status quo
B is a clear statement of the desired end state after the change
D are concrete steps towards the goal
X is the cost of the change

The equation can help headteachers to know where to 'apply their weight' to make a significant transformational change. First, it is essential to calculate the chances of success before embarking on commitment to transformation. This principle is eternal: as Jesus once asked,

> Which of you, when he wants to build a tower, does not first sit down and calculate the cost, to see if he has enough to complete it?

It was sound advice then, and it is sound advice now. Much energy, time and goodwill are required to make change happen so precious commodities should not be wasted upon futile exercises destined to fail. Calculating accurately the probability, C, that change will be successful is vital.

Early in this book I argued that the first step in transformational change is the creation of awareness of a sense of need. It is likely that the leader will feel it first in such strength as to contemplate the urgency of transformational change. Sense of need inevitably flows from dissatisfaction with the status quo and the probability of change being transformational is proportional to the level of dissatisfaction with the status quo. So the greater the value of A the higher the chance of making successful change.

B is about a clear understanding of where this is all leading. The better the grasp of the direction and the purpose, the higher the chances of success. Bennis and Nanus (1997) put it like this

> If there is a spark of genius in the leadership function at all, it must lie in a kind of magic, to assemble a clearly articulated vision of the future that is at once simple, easily understood, clearly desirable and energising.

It is within the power of leaders of schools to increase B by well-planned, creative communications that show the way. Bennis and Nanus developed these ideas further

> Leaders will have to be architects and cheerleaders for change: true visionaries who are able to point to destinations that are so desirable and credible that workers will enthusiastically become partners in making it happen.

Many people are addicted to the pleasures of travel and spend months working out where to go, how to get there, what sights to see and what pleasures to enjoy. Imagining a picture that is easily understood and clearly desirable is a powerful motivational force. When B is large, the chances of implementing successful change are high.

But successful change will happen only if there are credible outlines in place to make it happen. Visions are only transacted when decisive action plans are in place. The creation of the concrete steps to take was labelled D by Jacobs.

The combination of a strong dissatisfaction with the status quo, a destination so clearly focused that it is credible and desirable and a series of well thought out steps towards the desired end have to be more dominant in the minds of the transformational workforce than the cost incurred on the journey. The end has to be worth the effort.

Is the end worth the effort? Transformation is more probable when leaders are convinced and convincing that it is.

Different areas where transformation is needed

In an ever-changing educational world, the issues of concern change month by month, often through internal pressures on schools but also from externally imposed agendas. Amongst those generated by the latter is the issue of remodelling the workforce.

1. Remodelling the workforce

Once the little matter of funding to make the job possible is resolved, leaders will be faced with the enormous challenge of changing the face of traditional employment practice in their schools. Applying Jacobs' equation, it is plain that the probability of success depends on the level of dissatisfaction with the status quo. It is manifestly evident that teachers are dissatisfied with

> the pressure of their workload
>
> the absence of non-contact time (especially in primary)
>
> the burden of unnecessary clerical tasks.

It seems that A is high.

If we could see beyond the immediate funding complications, the horizon is filled with promise, a desired haven indeed. Teachers dream of a profession where

> *time is available to prepare well*
> *opportunity is created to plan*
> *developments with others*
> *students have better teacher contact*
> *teaching and learning become their*
> *priority.*

Most teachers I know try to work at the highest level at present, but will jump at a golden opportunity to enhance their professionalism in the name of greater service to young people with whom they are seeking to make a difference. It is difficult to imagine the benefits of being in places we have not yet seen, but teachers are beginning to believe that having time released from routine administrative duties to concentrate on teaching is more than a mirage in an arid desert; B is attractive.

However, D is a nightmare! How can the workforce be transformed? How will staff be recruited and trained? How does a headteacher overcome the problems of deterioration of behaviour (if it happens?) when teaching assistants supervise examinations? Handling issues like this is at the heart of transformational change. The principles outlined in this book help to address these matters.

A, B and D are high and may be seen as greater than the price that has to be paid. The National Union of Teachers has not been convinced at all and so hesitated about signing up to the agreement, and other unions are concerned lest the costs of implementation are beyond the scope of constrained budgets. In the end it seems that money will be provided to introduce transformation so massive that the face of education will be forever changed. A great deal is at stake. X is high – but the combination of A, B and D leaves me feeling that C is higher still. Ultimately transformation will happen and leaders are going to have to do it!

The opportunity is there to redesign the curriculum. There is enormous pressure to transform education after Key Stage 3 and also a growing movement, led by the *Times Educational Supplement* to 'target creativity' in primary schools.

2. Redesigning the curriculum

The government made plain that it requires a transformation of education post 14. This is not easy to do: some headteachers are concerned about

> the consequences of students being taught elsewhere
> the loss of control over students
> the quality of curriculum on offer
> the logistics and cost of wholesale movement
> the moral purpose behind some proposals.

However, there is dissatisfaction with the status quo. The Key Stage 4 curriculum, for instance, is widely regarded as restrictive, out-dated, de-motivating for many students and inappropriate to the twenty-first century. A is big.

The alternative possibility is both desirable and credible:

> Vocational education is valued
> Work in another institution could be re-energising for some students
> More appropriate courses are available
> Students will be more interested and engaged
> More students will achieve qualifications of which they are proud
> Collaboration between school and college will be helpful.

These are desirable, but are they credible? There are immense complications in putting plans in place but although it will take skill as well as high level communication and creativity it is achievable and so D can be considerable.

The issue of the cost (X) of such transformational change is high so schools will not be able to do it alone. Funding is coming on stream so it should be possible to demonstrate that A*B*D is greater than X, ergo transformation of the secondary agenda is possible.

It is unusual for the **Times Educational Supplement** to be so outspoken about the need for transformation in a specific area. In their campaign launched on 2 May 2003 their *Primary* editor, Diane Hofkins observed

> The overwhelming evidence is that the government's key stage 2 targets are becoming obstructive. They are no longer helping to raise standards, but are stifling opportunities for both teachers and children to be creative.

You may be sure there is an issue for transformation when Tim Brighouse weighs in with strident and typically pertinent observations:

> In Victorian times creativity was systematically extinguished through a

harsh system of 'payment by results'. According to a famous head of that period, 'the common idea of education...is of a set of memory trucks all in a row with navvies pitching ballast into them against time'. Sounds familiar doesn't it?

I do not believe that targets will be scrapped, though Charles Clarke has at least (some say at last) made some moves over the transformation of assessment. What seems certain is that creativity has to re-emerge: transformation is necessary. There is massive dissatisfaction in primary schools at the demise of creativity so A is high. No doubt primary schools would welcome renewed opportunity to re-engage with the Arts, Sport and the Humanities, while retaining the best of what has, until now, been the priority, Numeracy and Literacy. B is high too.

The *Times Educational Supplement* (2.5.03) is suggesting radical ideas:

> Be Bolshy: bin the targets and set your own
> Be Confident: bring back creativity and breadth
> Be Free: resist pressure to teach to tests.

These are the beginnings of an Action Plan. If schools take it up such a plan would need to be developed, but there is an embryo of a powerful D. Taken together, the popularity of such a move, the dissatisfaction with the status quo and the relatively easy creation of an action plan against no significant costs makes this a transformational winner.

There are substantial issues under consideration in many schools that have no external stimulus but where moves towards change are entirely generated from within, such as developing a culture of achievement.

3. Developing a Culture of Achievement

Whether the desire to develop a culture of achievement would exist without published league tables is an interesting question. But the fact remains that achievement is of fundamental importance to most leaders. Jacobs' simple equation can be applied to analysing the possibility of change.

Dissatisfaction with the status quo does not always exist where it ought to and this leads to coasting schools. Leaders, aware of comparability figures, may have work to do to establish a sense of dissatisfaction with their performance. Feeling the need and facing the brutal facts remain the starting points. It ought to be easy to make B high, but complacency may need to be challenged and this is done best by creating the sense of need. This process may require

    revealing the facts about a school
    demonstrating comparability
    illustrating potential that is being
    unrealised
    discussing the consequences of
    retaining the status quo.

The probability of change is highly dependent on a significant value of A but this may not be easily achieved. Were it not that some teachers think that their present achievement is the promised land, it would be easy to enthuse the staff about a future where

    students' examination results are
    higher
    opportunities for further education
    are enhanced
    families are happier and feel better
    because of evident success
    staff feel successful, energised by
    their contribution to raising
    achievement.

Once A and B are resolved, action planning D is straightforward. Planning will need care, precision, detail, accountability structures and follow

through, but it is not nearly as problematic as A and B.

The cost (X) of making this transformation should not be underestimated and it may take extended, open consultation to address dissatisfaction levels. This can be done through staff conferences, bringing in guest speakers who will open up the issue and allowing quality time to deal with vital issues. After that, the costs incurred in promoting achievement in students and staff are likely to be investment in time for key people focused on making it happen, funding for faculties and departments to look at schemes of work and developing student achievement and financing imaginative, creative challenges for the students that have commensurate rewards. These costs are high and will be a serious argument for resistance unless A and B have been developed in the hearts and minds of teachers.

Developing a culture of achievement will make the school a happier and more vibrant environment. It will create a momentum so that success breeds more success and it will release students from the shackles of low aspiration to dream of goals they would never have thought possible. It is a transformational change of immense importance.

4. Creating an Ethos for Learning

All other issues fall behind this central requirement for good education yet it is commonly known that there are schools where the ethos is unconducive to learning, where there is poor behaviour, disengagement of students, bullying, disorder and truancy. Rarely is this admitted until all this is transformed and then some of the awful truth is revealed. During recent research I have met five headteachers whose initial work involved restoring some sort of order to a school that was almost out of control. St. George's, Maida Vale is one highly publicised example. The second chapter of Lady Marie Stubbs' book was headed 'Could it get any worse?' Even allowing for poetic licence, the evidence she cites is alarming:

- an unsettled, frenetic feeling to the school

- regular episodes of fighting and violence

- unruly, disobedient young people

- attendance well below 90%

- poor timekeeping by both students and staff

- verbal abuse of staff by students

- low staff morale

- young people inattentive in lessons

- over-casual dress and demeanour, students appear careless

- an air of resignation and pessimism among staff

These are characteristics of schools facing troubled times. They are places where supply teachers will not return, where the daily battle leaves staff feeling demoralised and depressed and where achievement is less the issue than survival.

Yet schools like this are being transformed. The probability of change in such schools depends on A, the level of dissatisfaction within it, particularly at leadership level. There will undoubtedly be dissatisfaction among some students and parents and in the staff room but none of them are in a strong position to make change. Ofsted reports on schools of this kind inevitably comment that leadership is a source of concern yet the overwhelming feeling in the school is of denial rather than dissatisfaction, denial which thrives on excuses paraded as reasons and a stance that 'it's them, not us'. 'Them' can be any combination of the LEA, the governors, the students, the socially disadvantaged background or the government. All these play some

part, but those who will make the transformational change are the leaders working with their team. If A is high it is likely that there will be the will to tackle the problem. Leaders owe it to teachers to check their perceptions of 'how things are'. In most schools if staff are asked what could be better they will say discipline but in many schools that is actually the case. It might be a huge problem yet the school leaders still refuse to accept that something must be done. Depressingly, some schools labour on with staff badly dissatisfied and disillusioned and leaders appearing to believe that all is well. To create change A has to be high at the top! Resistance to change can actually come from the leadership since to admit dissatisfaction seems to imply failure, inability to do one's job, damages self-esteem and challenges a sense of competence. This is why new leadership sometimes has to be parachuted in.

The alternative desired end B is not difficult to define. All most parents want for their children is

- order in classrooms so that learning is possible

- the security of a safe environment in which to learn

- a school where the teachers care about their children

- an educational centre which they call 'our school'

- opportunity to learn lessons about life and good citizenship

All of us can tell horrendous tales about maverick extreme parents but in the main, parents see a desired end very clearly. So do teachers. What they want is

- an orderly school environment

- disruptive young people appropriately dealt with to minimise their effect on other students

- support when they are struggling with difficult young people

- an opportunity to work with students rather than battling with them

Teachers know they have their part to play but many believe the quality of their working environment is determined by those in school leadership. In his research into the impact of the Numeracy and Literacy strategies, Michael Fullan concluded that '*success on a large scale had a strong degree of front-end, assertive, top-down leadership*'. I believe that to be true for setting the atmosphere in schools too. Leaders need to be clear that where they want to go is where the staff would like them to be. This issue of school ethos is enormously important – B needs to be clear for successful transformational change. It could be argued that this process is easier in some geographical areas than others. That may be, but it is abundantly evident that some schools in challenging areas have a splendid ethos so it can be done, wherever we are.

Once a leader has decided to tackle this issue of school ethos, it is straightforward to put in place some concrete steps. Marie Stubbs gave some excellent examples:

- Smarten up the environment

In her case it meant mounting attractive displays, creating games areas in the playground and making a warm and welcoming entrance area.

- Strengthen the emphasis on working atmosphere

School uniform was regarded as important because it created the impression of purposeful endeavour but the main emphasis was to make the benefits of learning a subject of regular discussion.

- Give responsibility to students

Though meeting with some resistance from teachers, the headteacher allowed students to stay in school at breaks and lunchtimes. She provided chairs and seats in designated areas for student use and spent time there with her senior leadership team talking to students. She created prefects. Giving responsibility was not abused – it rarely is.

- Sort out the flash points

Recognising where the trouble usually happens is not difficult. Removing the opportunity for problems to arise is far better than addressing them when they have occurred. The local police were invited to have a presence at the gates after school, not to sort out problems but to prevent them.

- Show trust in students

Following much encouragement, guidance and support to students about behaviour expected at St. George's, Marie Stubbs was able to walk in the school playground with her small grandchild without fear or concern. In any large school there will be some who let you down; it is important not to allow such students to determine the ethos and practice of the community.

- Provide high quality support staff

Behaviour support specialists are capable of offering guidance and support to students and of advising and helping staff on how to handle difficult situations. Any truly comprehensive school will have some young people with serious behavioural problems and some may be beyond the experience and skills of teachers. Specialist support is costly but it is invaluable.

- Patrol the patch

At Nunthorpe we have a senior colleague who 'walks and whistles' so this means that staff know when they hear him that he is on their corridor to help and support. Senior staff wandering the school are not wasting time but setting and enforcing standards. Staff should not feel they are being checked up on, though this is almost inevitable. When I visit classes I always emphasise that it is the students who I am there to see and I ask 'Is there anything about this class that I need to know, please?' Students know that I have this routine and know too that if the report is bad something will be done.

- Let them know you care

Marie Stubbs consciously attempted to make clear that students and staff were valued and important and deserved the best. People are not prepared to believe the rhetoric if it is not matched by actions that convey the same message.

These examples all show that D can be provided. There are concrete steps towards the desired end. A, B and D are all high, and so is X, the cost of change.

Such transformation of ethos costs money and resources so needs to be treated as a priority. No school can ever be successful unless the ethos is right. It will certainly cost time, energy, sacrifice and determination. The importance of the issue means that it is worth paying.

These four illustrations of areas of potential transformation are selected from many possibilities. However, each potential transformational opportunity can measured in terms of Jacobs' equation to determine the likelihood of success. Knowing where to put one's weight is a matter of great importance. Albert Einstein worked on the following principle,

> I soon learned to scent out that which was able to lead to fundamentals and to turn aside everything else, from the multitude of things that clutter up the mind and divert from the essential.

Transformational leaders take the same approach.

Chapter 11

We're not all brilliant

You've never met an ordinary person.
CS Lewis

Headteachers are a mixed ability group of people as observed by Jane Phillips in the *Times Educational Supplement* in May 2003,

> In an ideal world, all heads would be superlative and, if they were not, parachuting in a 'super head' would solve all problems.
>
> But we live in the real world – and we know there is a normal distribution among heads and that the command-style importation of super heads just does not work.
>
> The majority of heads range from competent to good to excellent. These heads will perform better in an atmosphere of trust and where their governors offer them both support and challenge.

Jane Phillips is Chair of the National Association of Governors and Managers and her views will be welcomed by most headteachers for common sense and realism.

Because we are not all brilliant does not mean that we cannot all improve and move forward – that was the theme of *Heading Towards Excellence,* Rowling (2002) which outlined a process for moving forwards. However, transformational change is not all about *one* person's leadership quality or style. Harris and Lambert (2003) point out that

> As long as improvement is dependent on a single person or a few people or outside directions or forces, it will fail.

Schools, and the people in them, have a propensity to depend too much on a strong head or other authority figures for direction and guidance.

Leaders who do not have charismatic personalities can make transitional change happen by

- seeking talent from within the school to lead aspects of change

- appointing leaders with complementary skills to their own

- adjusting leadership structures to take account of teacher's strengths

- sharing responsibility by sub-dividing action plans

Research shows that highly capable individuals have to be careful not to leave a situation that will deteriorate on their departure. The goal is not entrepreneurial achievement but enduring achievement.

When I was visiting Corbridge in Northumberland, I was amused by an advertisement for socks in a shop window that said, 'Everlasting socks, guaranteed six months'. Leadership that is entrepreneurial can prove to be equally short-lived. The characteristics of entrepreneurial leadership, often relying on one dynamic leader, are shown in the box below and compared with those whose leadership leads to enduring transformation. In the transformation that really makes the difference, the change agents are scattered throughout the organisation and not in just one office. Though headteachers are from a mixed ability group, there are skills that all of them can learn that will lead to genuine transformation.

The highest class of leader according to Collins (2001) is what he calls a Level 5 executive and defines as a 'leader who builds enduring greatness through a paradoxical blend of personal humility and professional will' so charisma is not an issue. Achievement at the enduring level is possible if the right structures and processes are in place. What a leader does need, however, are two qualities, namely:

Ferocious resolve and absolute commitment

Ferocious resolve was what Collins called professional will. He defined it as 'an almost stoic determination to do whatever needs to be done to make the organisation great'. You don't have to be charismatic to be determined! As for Absolute Commitment, Bennis (1999) maintained that the 'time and energy devoted to the (transformational) work demand a commitment and conviction bordering on love'.

Entrepreneurial	v	Enduring
A few leaders at the the top	v	Leaders at every level
Seek efficiency	v	Seek Efectiveness
Lead by allocating resources	v	Lead by creating alliances
React and adapt to change	v	Anticipate, create and plan the future
Strongly hierarchical	v	Diverse, collegial and collaborative
Direct and supervise individuals	v	Empower and inspire teams
Hold information closely	v	Share information widely
Leader as boss	v	Leader as coach
Develop good administrators	v	Develop future leaders

Michael Eisner of the Disney Corporation called this quality a 'strong point of view', or POV in Hollywood speak. Eisner believes that it is always the person with conviction who wins the day. Bennis reckoned that in Hollywood POV is worth at least 80 IQ points. And in schools Absolute Commitment is worth a great many IQ points.

John Parker Stewart argues in his presentation entitled Team of Champions that transformational change leaders possess four characteristics that do not relate to charismatic personality directly, nor are they the sole prerogative of strong leaders. The qualities he identified are

1. Leaders listen effectively for ideas, attitudes and feelings of their people and they handle what they hear professionally

2. Leaders build a spirit of trust. Team members have the support they need to take risks and make good decisions when leaders are honest and truthful.

3. Leaders empower their people to act. They clarify tasks, provide needed resources and then support and protect team members.

4. Leaders use humour to maintain a balance between expecting results and creating a pleasant workplace environment.

It is clear that headteachers and leaders of varying abilities are able to devise ways to fulfil these four liberating tasks. What needs to be avoided is what Alma Harris (2003) calls 'trait theory' – the idea that 'if only our headteacher possessed certain traits, we would have good leadership'. Traits are often a personal interpretation of what leadership is, made by those who hold varying views. This 'trait theory' is unhelpful. As Harris says,

> This tendency has caused those who might have rolled up their sleeves and

Absolute Commitment is worth 80 IQ points

pitched in to help to abstain from the work of leadership, thereby abdicating both responsibilities and their opportunities.

Headteachers should not let themselves be victims of trait supporters, nor should they be perpetrators of the theory: many a headteacher has expectations of the style of operation of Heads of Department, for example, which has the same stultifying effect as Harris so graphically describes.

Where ought a leader to begin?
It may be best to begin by asking some key questions:

1. What am I passionate about?

2. Will what I am passionate about make a difference in my school?

3. Using Jacobs' equation, is it likely to be successful?

4. Will success be significant?

5. Do I want this to be our priority?

What am I passionate about?
There are many areas in which transformation is possible and these will vary from school to school. When making choices, the guiding direction may be indicated by asking 'what am I passionate about?' The matters which excite our passion are likely to receive our enthusiasm, commitment, dedication, expenditure of energy and love.

Jim Collins and his team recognised that companies that became great often had a simple idea on which they focused almost totally. They called it the Hedgehog Concept based on Isaiah Berlin's famous parable about the hedgehog and the fox. The researchers discovered that there were three underlying principles that guided companies to greatness. These are shown in modified form in the three circles shown below.

Will what I am passionate about make a difference?

This brings us back to Fullan's moral purpose. It is so central to transformational change because it is motivating and empowering. A careful and calculated audit needs to be done of our activity profile within schools so that we might avoid what Stephen Covey (1989) called being 'deep in the thick of thin things'. There are many thin things around, all capable of absorbing hours of time and sapping energy and vitality. What makes a difference and what I am passionate about are excellent filters for determining our choices.

Is what I choose to focus on likely to be successful?

With passion and moral purpose behind it, any idea has a good chance but the Jacobs' test is worth applying: how do other people feel about the present position, and how much do they desire the projected end?

Will success be significant?

Significance is difficult to define, not least because it varies from one person to the next. In the context of transformational change, making it happen will be significant if:

- a positive difference is made for students

- most teachers feel fulfilled and energised

- values and moral purposes are advanced

- the community is enriched by the change

- in some ways, lives are improved by the transformation

- you, and others, feel good about your achievement.

Recognising what we are good at, giving ourselves to it and developing at the same time, engaging in what we believe is worth the while are all excellent practice. Seeing an undertaking through to a desired end is likely to offer a deep sense of significance.

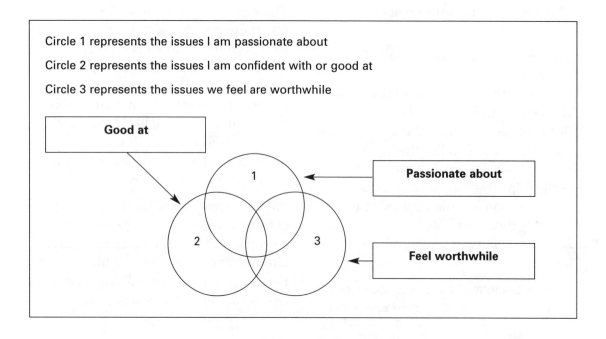

Circle 1 represents the issues I am passionate about

Circle 2 represents the issues I am confident with or good at

Circle 3 represents the issues we feel are worthwhile

Do I want this to be a priority?

The thin things of life have siren voices, beguiling, bewitching and diverting. It is up to transformational leaders at all levels to identify priorities and be single minded. Stephen Covey (1989) attempted to clarify the issue of prioritising. The diagram below is adapted from his work.

It is possible to categorise most activities in order of urgency and importance. Covey's advice is that matters both important and urgent should have priority: he allows for most serious consideration to be given to matters which are important but not urgent. The danger always arises when the demands made by the urgent create an insistence all their own demanding time and attention now. Determined leaders know it is wisest to concentrate on the priority issues.

The clarion call of other issues should be disregarded. Peter Drucker tackled this issue too and said *doing deals (off focus things) is a much more exciting way to spend your day than doing actual work.*

We never stop learning

One head I admire greatly refuses to be beguiled by meetings with the great and the good because his vision is for transformational change in student behaviour and staff commitment. He chose to sacrifice 'the exciting way to spend my days', in favour of establishing the heart of his vision with his team. It paid handsome dividends and the staff and students felt good.

In review of Bennis and Thomas's (2002) *Geeks and Geezers* George Schulz wrote that; *As a Geezer, I still want to understand leadership better – not just how to lead but also how to follow the best people.*

Recently I was involved with a telephone conference among 13 people. As part of the introductions we were invited to say who we were and what we had done in our schools that led to our being included in that group. I found it difficult and humbling: it seemed that everybody

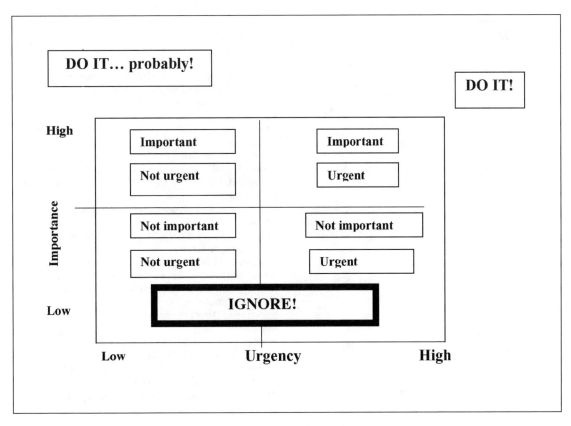

had done so much more than I had. Maybe they had but that is not the point. What I have discovered is that reading about and talking with people who have achieved great things helps me to move my leadership forward little by little.

The authors of *Geeks and Geezers* put it like this

> The ability to learn is a defining characteristic of being human: the ability to continue learning is an essential art of leadership.

Leaders are a mixed ability group of people but we can all take time and trouble to be lifelong learners. Even if we feel ordinary, we can choose to take the lead from Oscar Wilde:

> We are all in the gutter, but some of us are looking at the stars.

References

Adair J. (1998) *Effective Leadership*, Pan
Adair J. (2002) *Effective Strategic Leadership*, Macmillan
Albrecht K. (1994) *The Northbound Train*, AMACOM
Beare H. (2001) *Creating the Future School*, Routledge Falmer
Bennis W. (1994) *On becoming a Leader*, Addison Wesley
Bennis W. and Nanus B. (1997) *Leaders*, Harper Business
Bennis W. and Thomas R.J. (2002) *Geeks and Geezers*, HBS Press
Black J. and Gregersen H. (2002) *Leading Strategic Change*, Prentice Hall
Bossidy L. and Charan R. (2002) *Execution: The Discipline of Getting Things Done*, Random House
Boyett J and Boyett J. (1998) *The Guru Guide*, Wiley
Branson R. (2002) *Losing my Virginity*, Virgin
Brown A.D. (1999) *The Six Dimensions of Leadership*, Random House
Collins J. (2001) *Good to Great*, Random House
Collins J.C. and Porras J.I. (1995) *Building a Visionary Company*, California Management Review
Covey S. (1989) *The 7 habits of highly effective people*, Simon and Schuster
De Bono E. (1999) *New Thinking for the New Millennium*, Viking
De Bono. (1999) *Six Thinking Hats*, Penguin
DePree M. (1992) *Leadership Jazz*, Doubleday
Drucker P. (1996) *Leadership – Can it be Learned?* Forbes
Earl L. and Katz S. (2002) *Leading Schools in a Data Rich World*, Kluwer
Fullan M. (2001) *Leading in a Culture of Change*, Jossey-Bass
Fullan M. (2003) *Education in Motion*, in partnership with Leannta
Gardner J. (1990) *On Leadership*, New York Press
Gladwell M. (2000) *The Tipping Point*, Boston: Little Brown
Guiliani R. (2002) *Guiliani*, Little Brown
Goleman D. (1996) *Emotional Intelligence: Why it can matter more than IQ*, Bloomsbury
Harris A. and Lambert L. (2003) *Building Leadership Capacity for School Improvement*, OUP
Jacobs R. (1994) *Real Time Strategic Change*, Berrett-Koehler
Koestenbaum P. (2002) *Leadership – The Inner Side of Greatness*, Jossey-Bass
Kotter J. (1996) *Leading Change*, HBS Press
Kotter J. (2002) *The Heart of Change*, HBS Press
Parsons R. (2002) *The Heart of Success*, Hodder and Stoughton
Macbeath J. and Myers K. (1999) *Effective School Leaders*, Prentice Hall
Maxwell J.C. (1998) *The 21 Irrefutable Laws of Leadership*, Nelson
Morgan G. (1997) *Images of Organisation*, Sage
Nanus B. (1992) *Visionary Leadership*, Jossey-Bass
Rowling J.R. (2002) *Heading Towards Excellence*, Trentham Books
Secretan L. (1996) *Reclaiming the Higher Ground*, Macmillan
Stoll L., Fink D. and Earl L. (2003) *It's about Learning (and it's about time)* Routledge Falmer
Stubbs M. (2003) *Ahead of the Class*, John Murray
Welch J. (2001) *Jack*, Headline
Woodruff W. (1999) *The Road to Nab End*, Abacus